May your imagination soar with every stroke of color you add to these pages. Each line is an invitation to explore the wonders of your creativity.
May this book be a canvas for your dreams, a sanctuary for your thoughts, and a celebration of your vibrant spirit.
With love and endless encouragement.

This book is dedicated with much love and care to my stepdaughter Maria Thereza.

LOVE U

Lelo Abud
2024

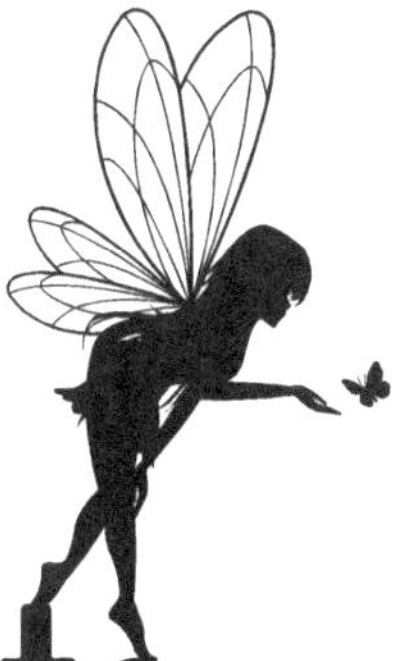

This book belongs to

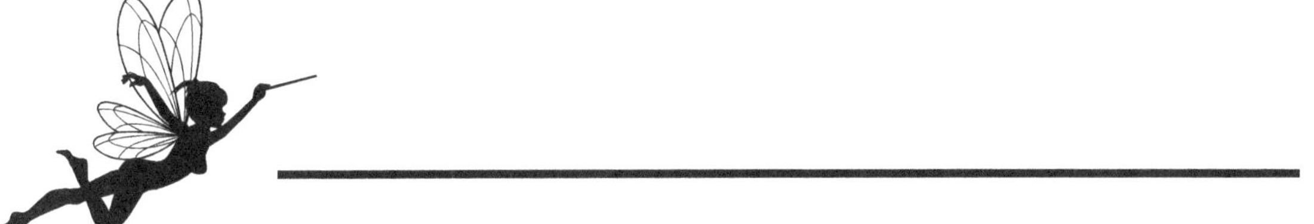

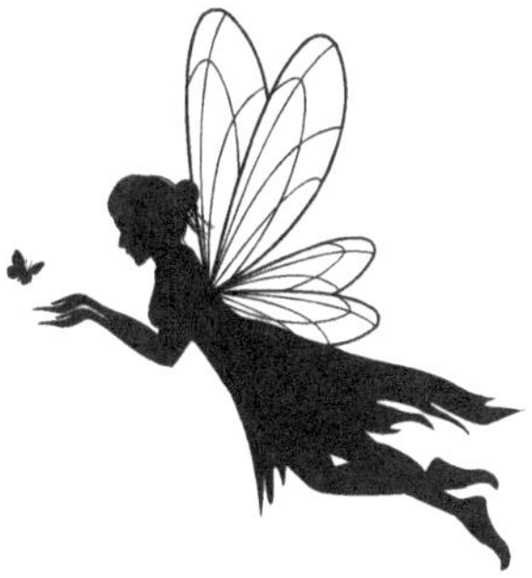

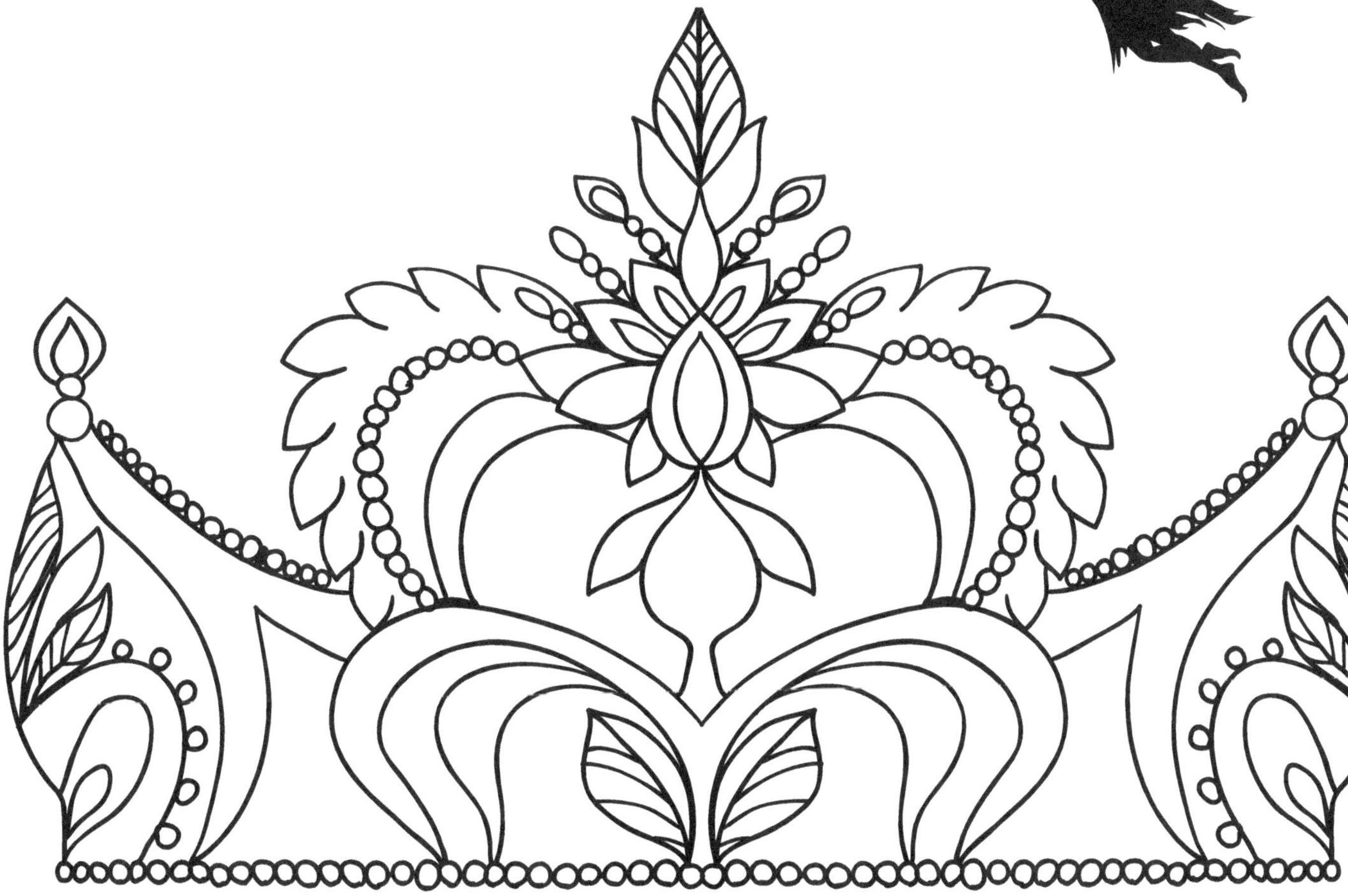

____

Test Color

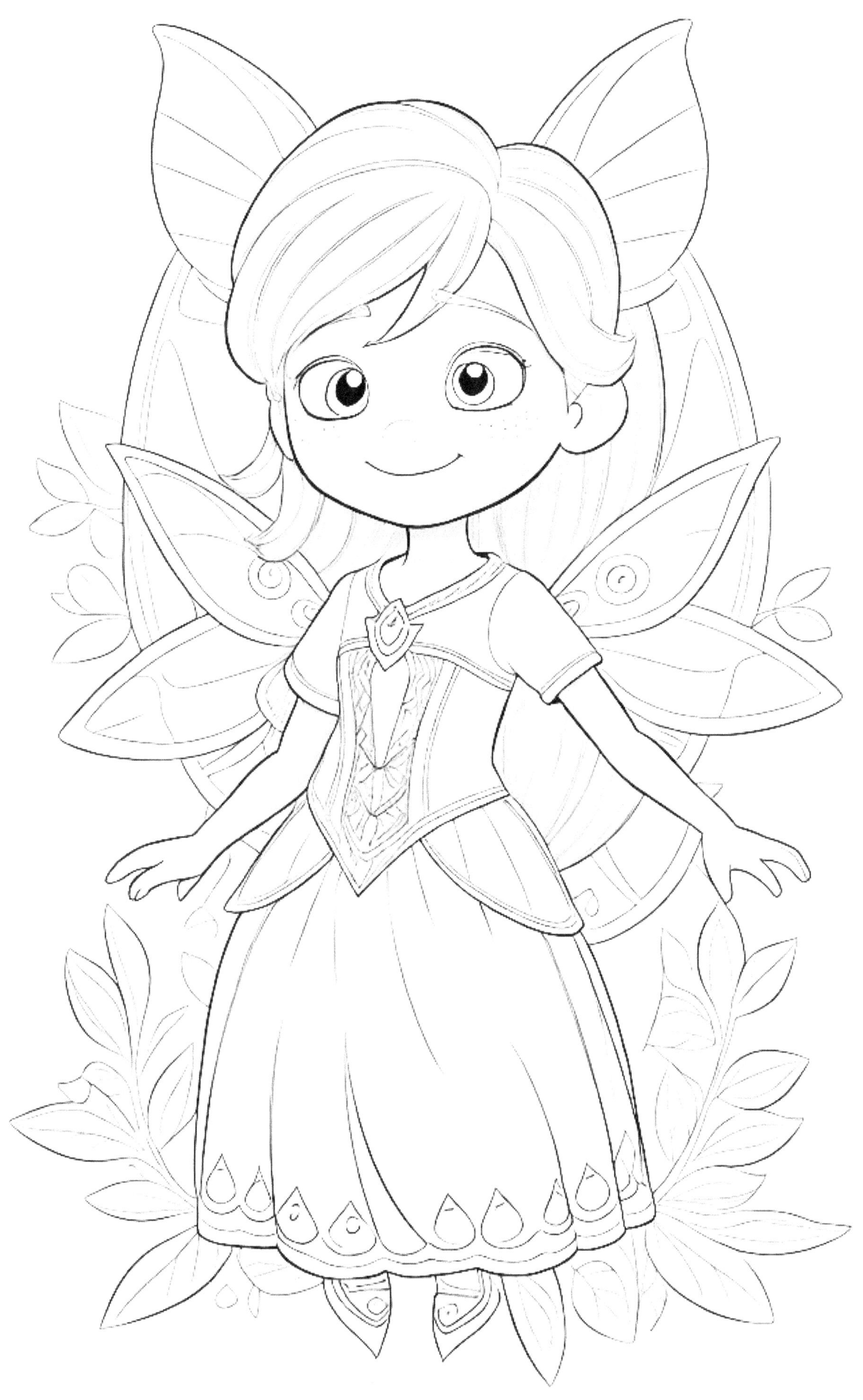

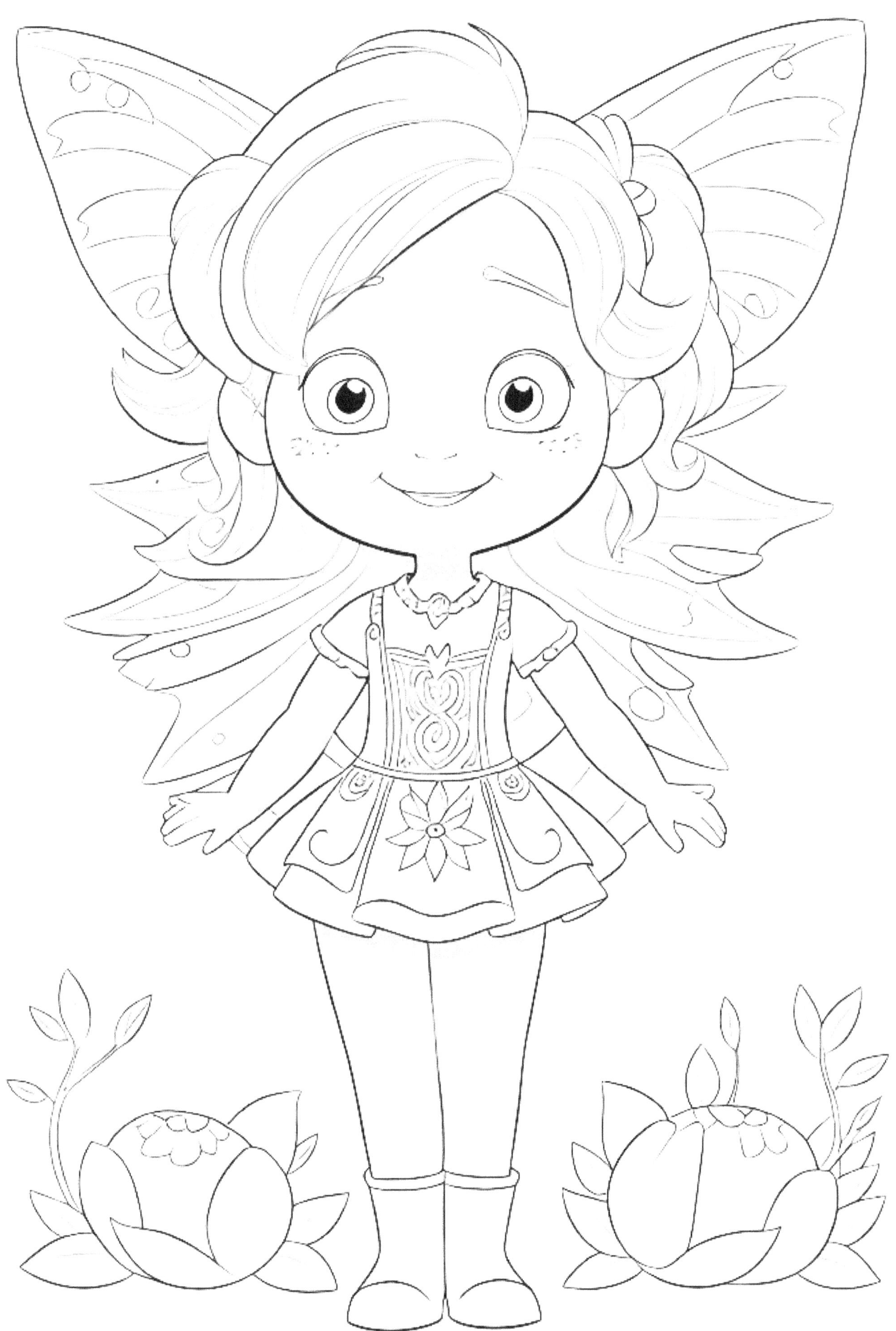

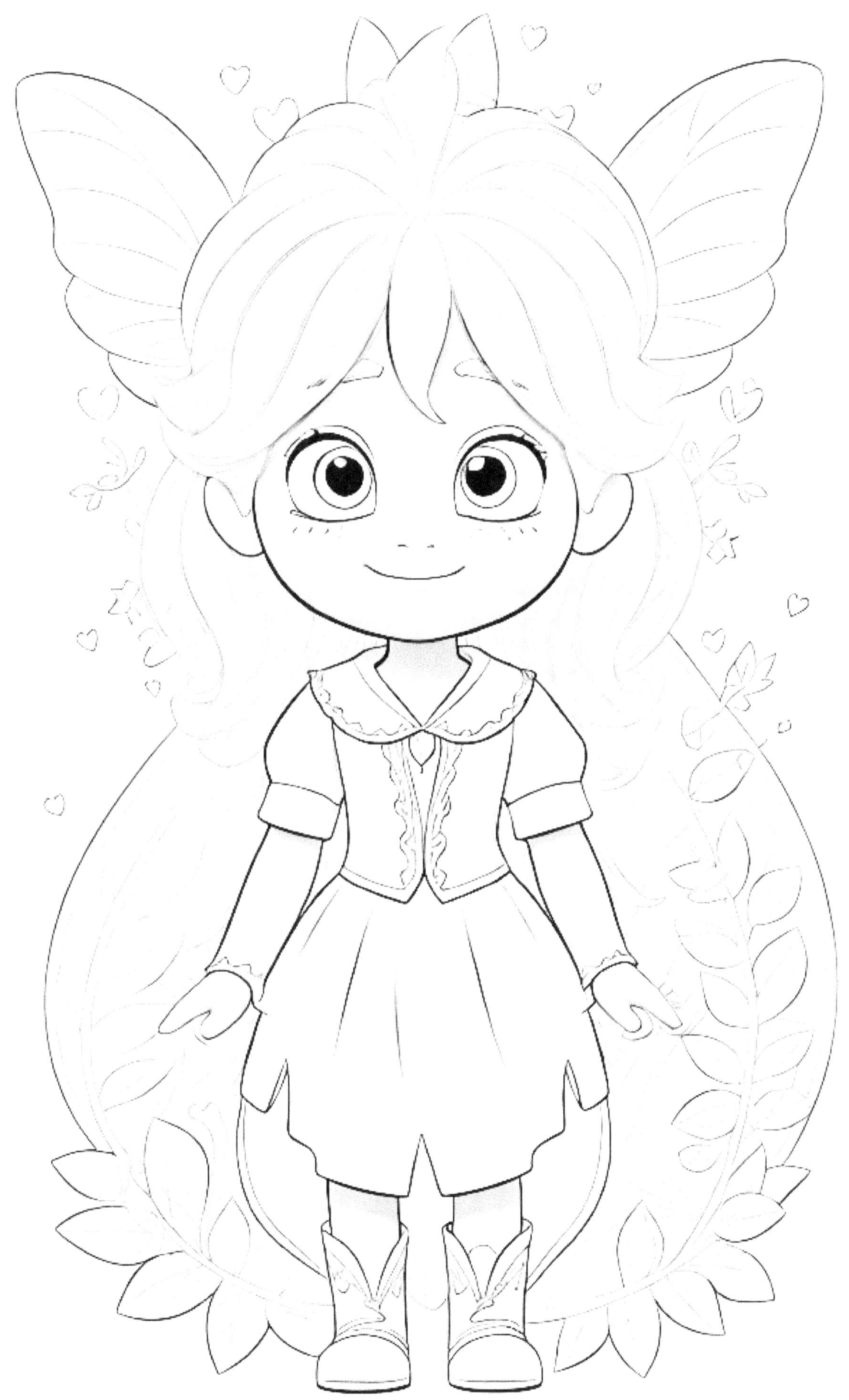

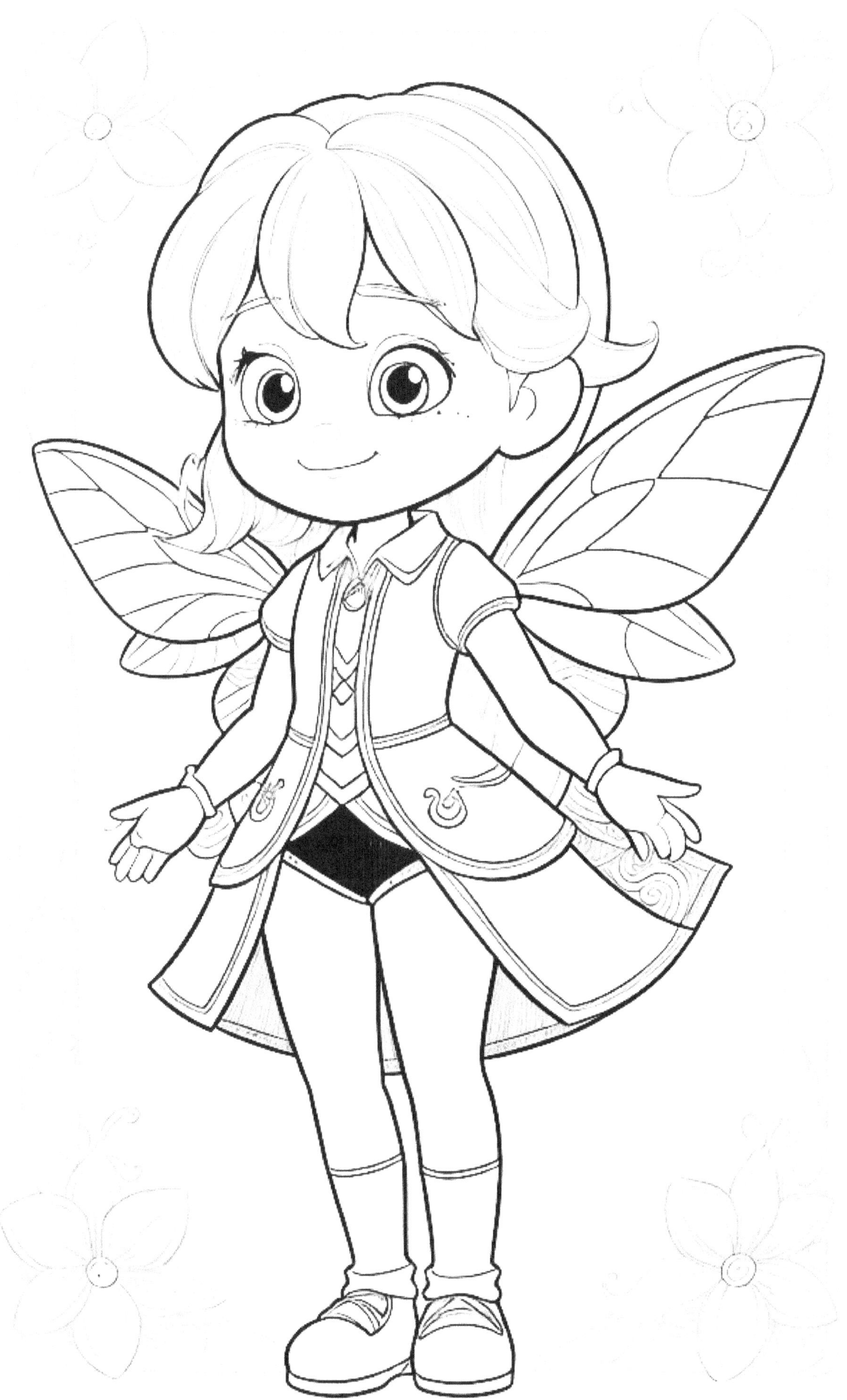

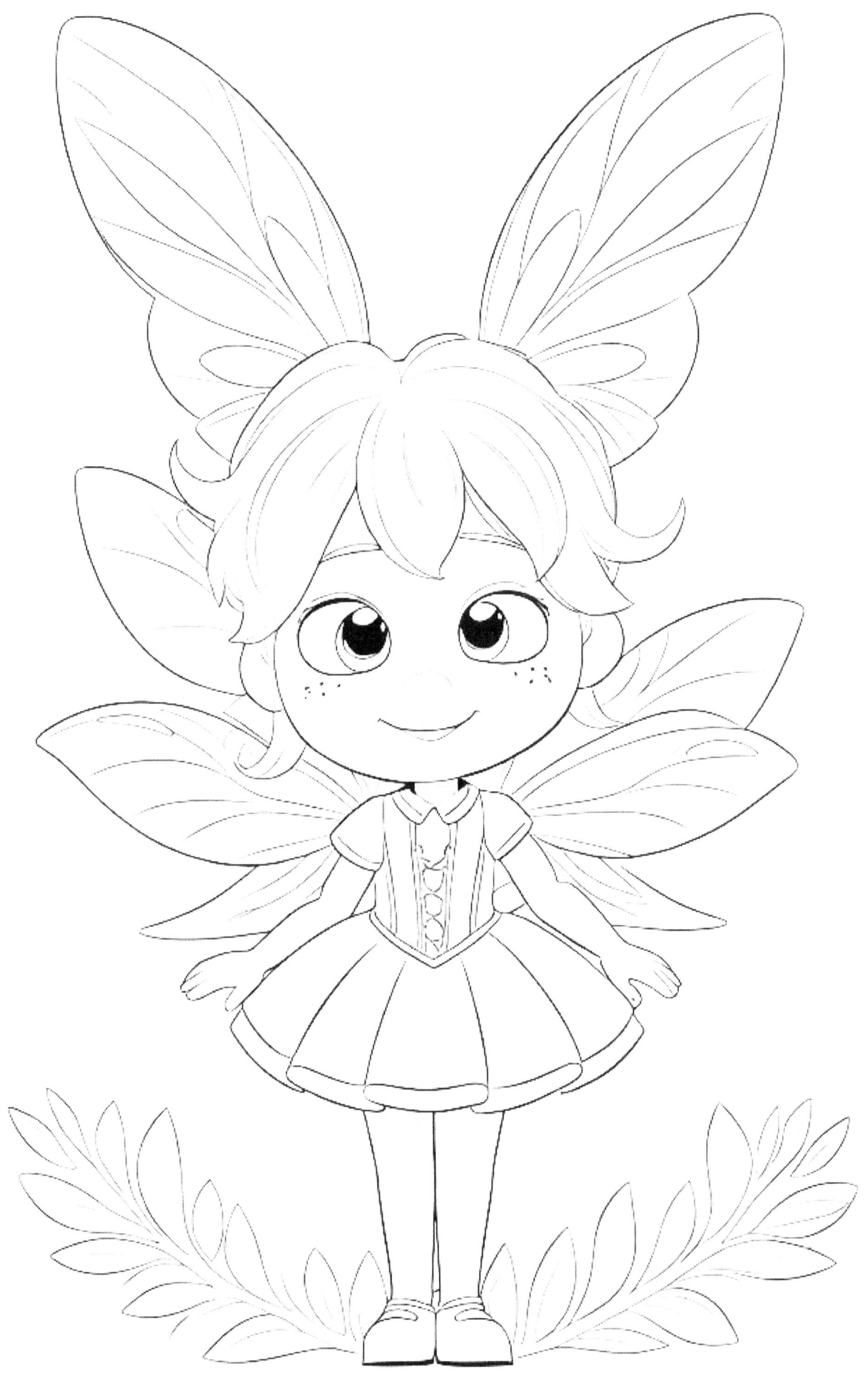

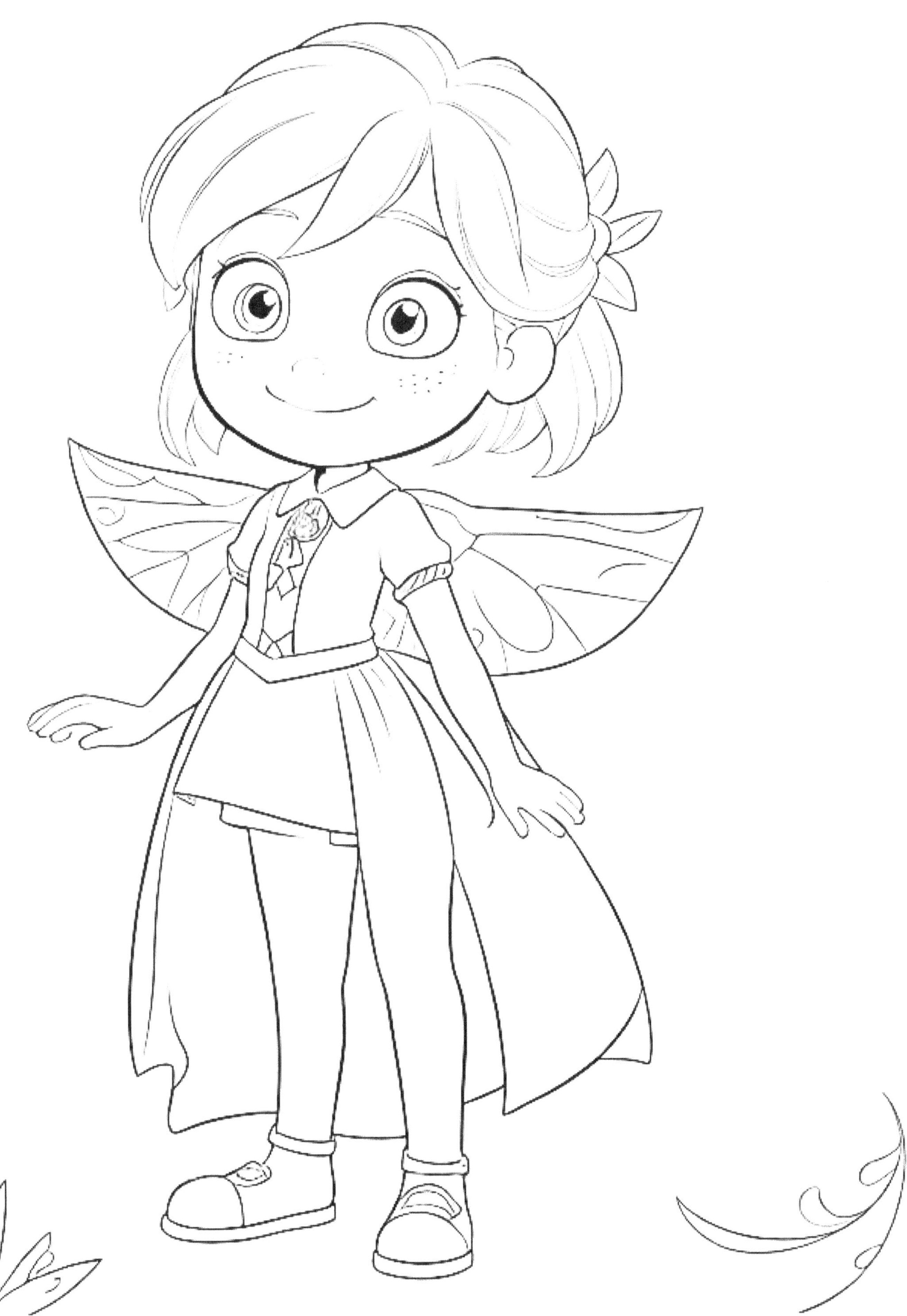

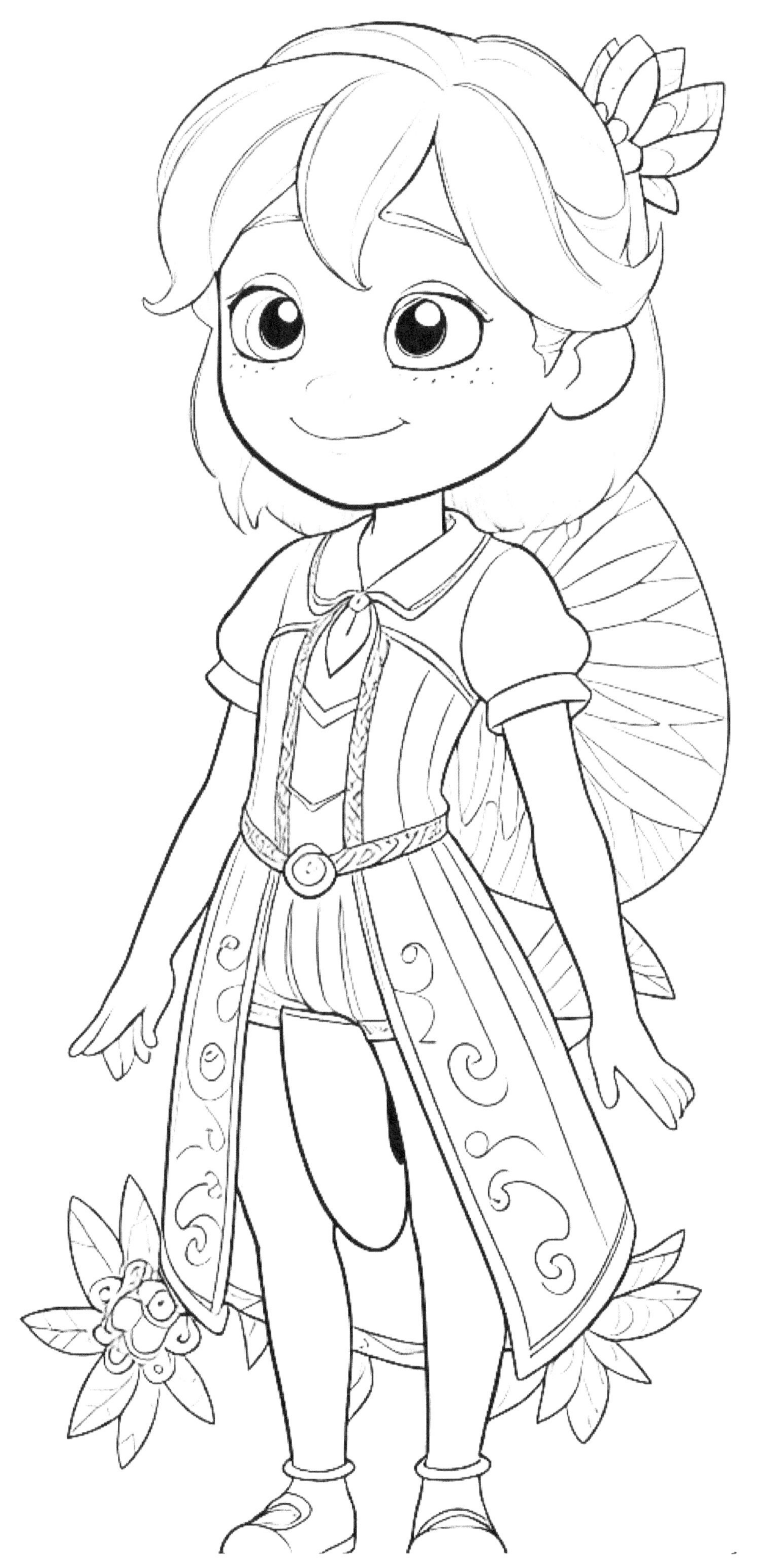

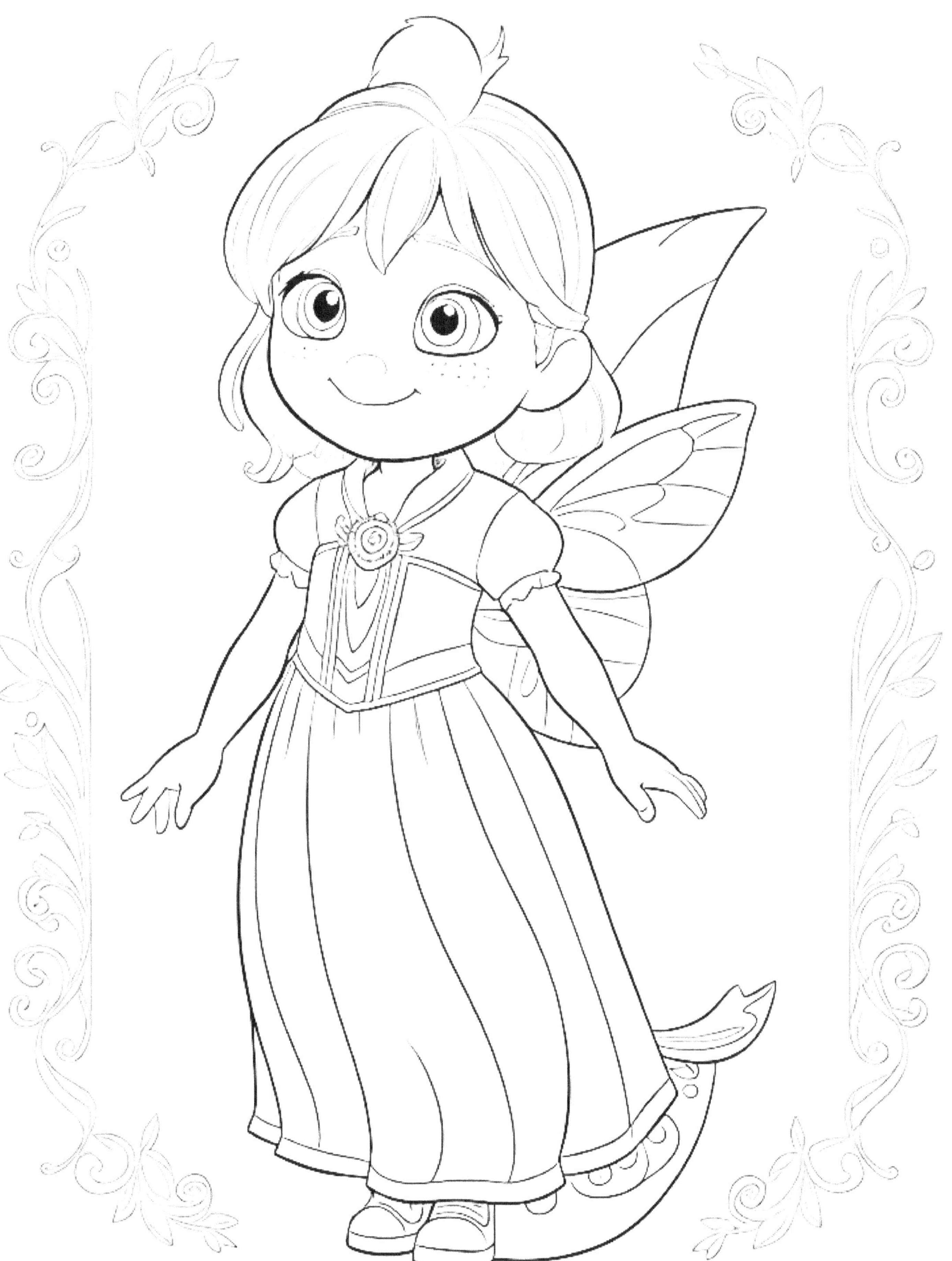

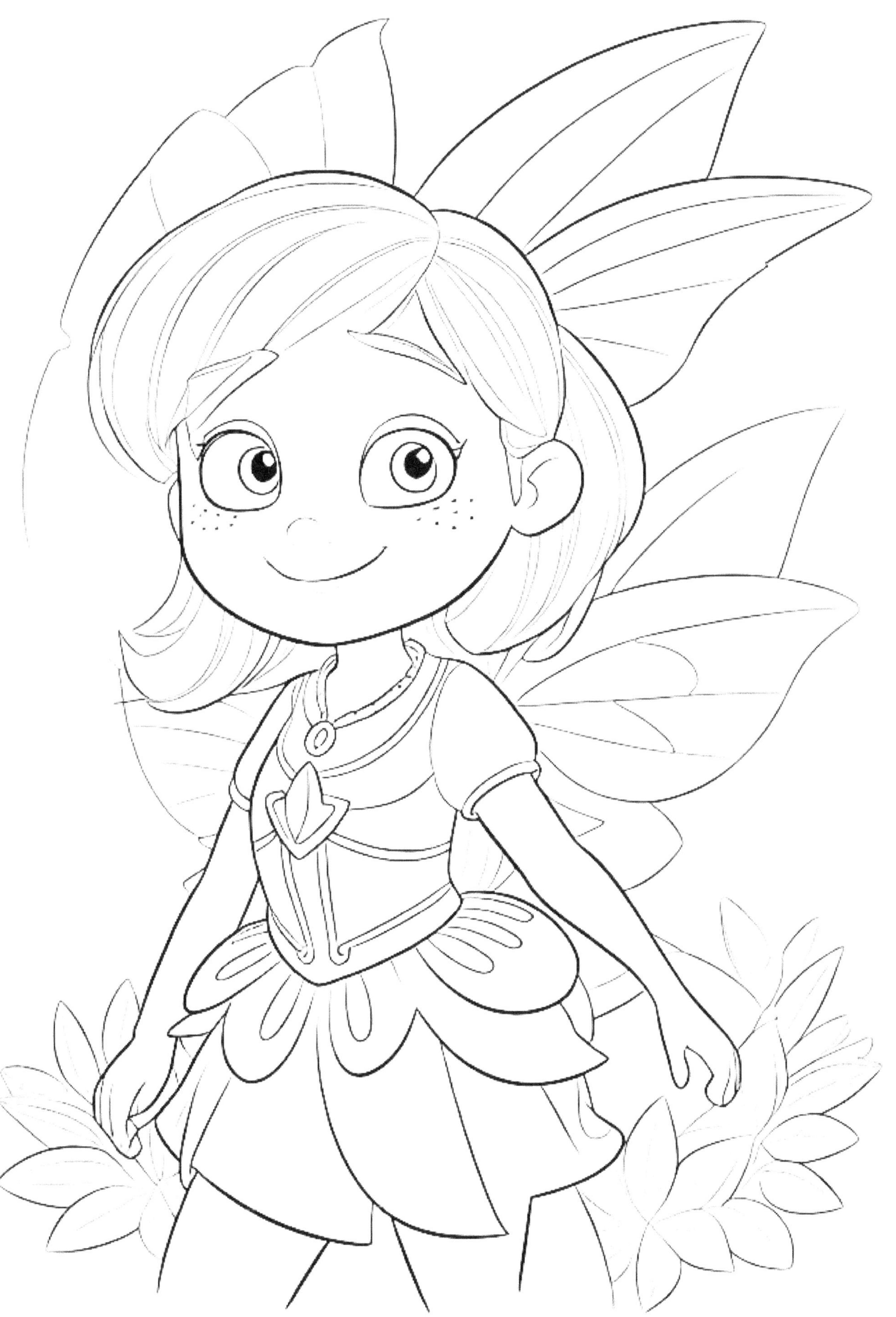

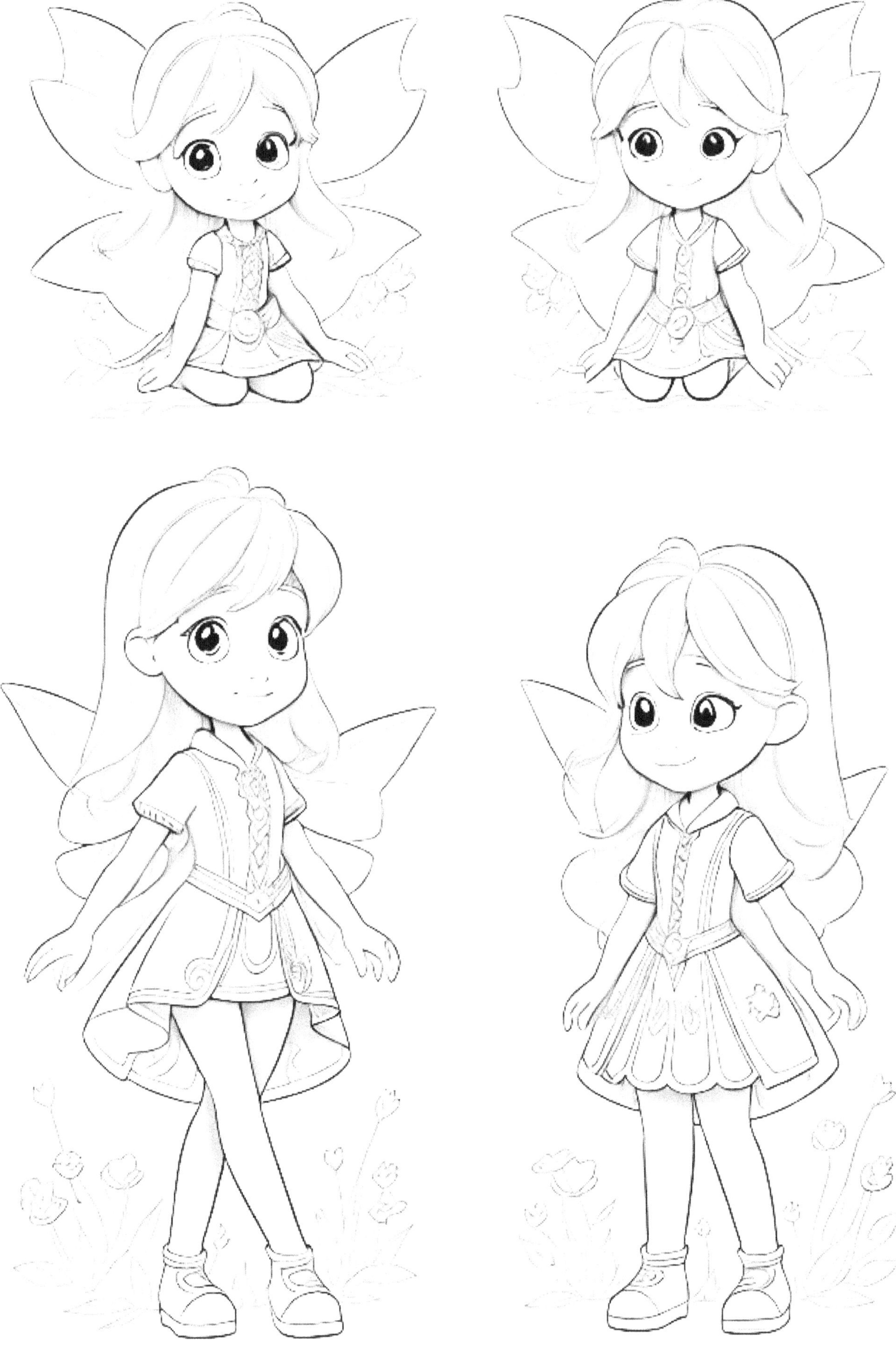

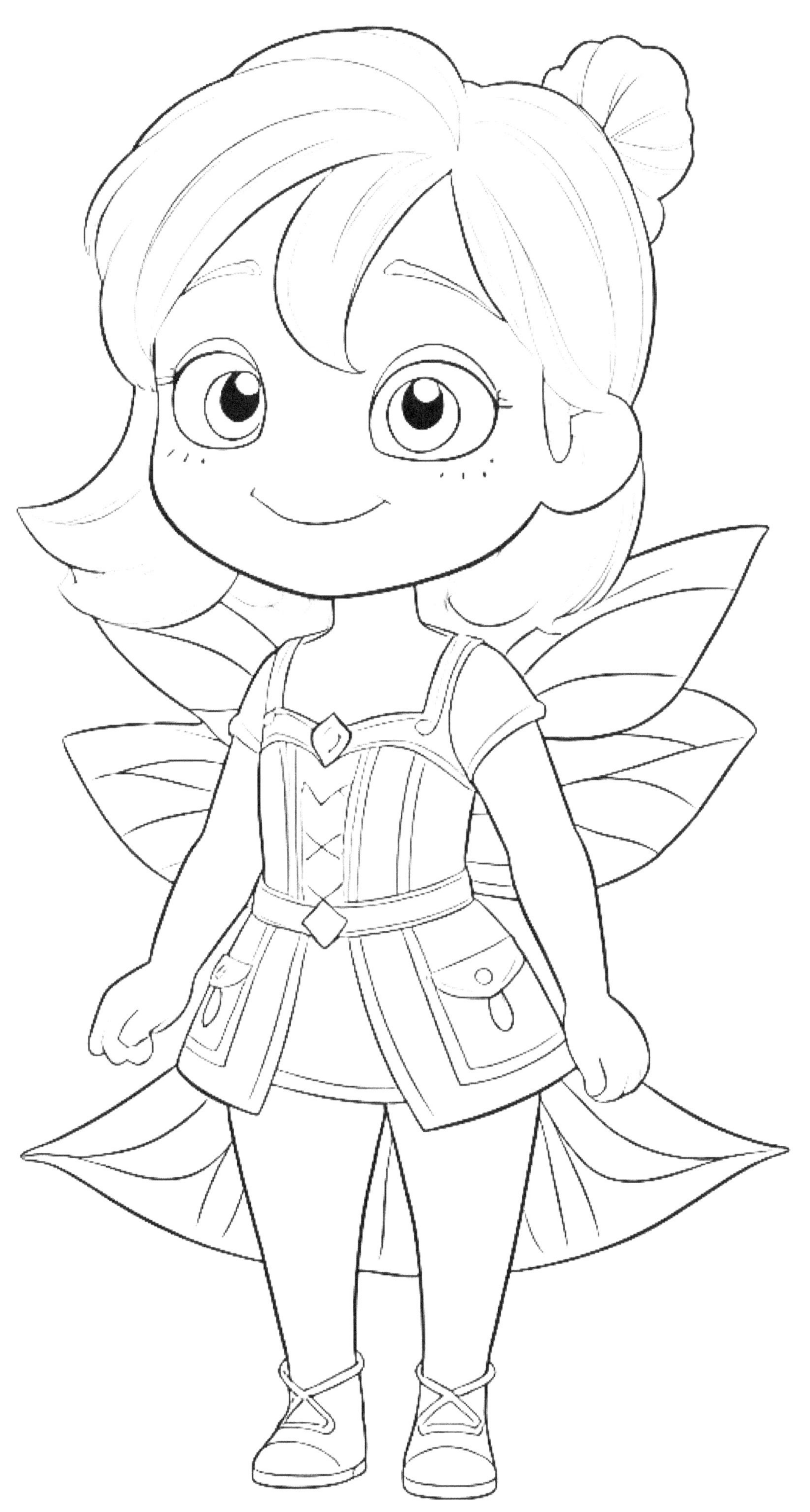

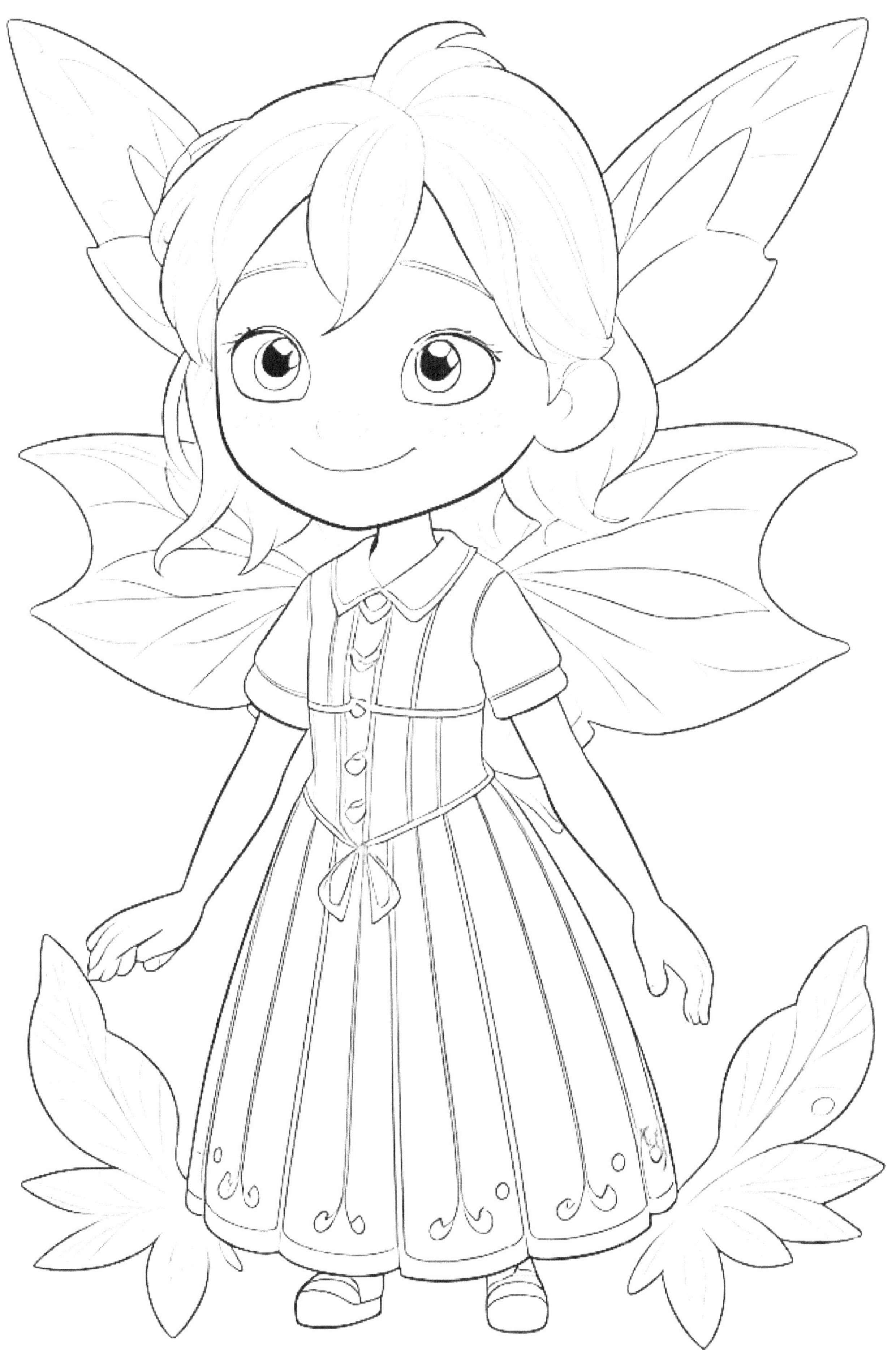

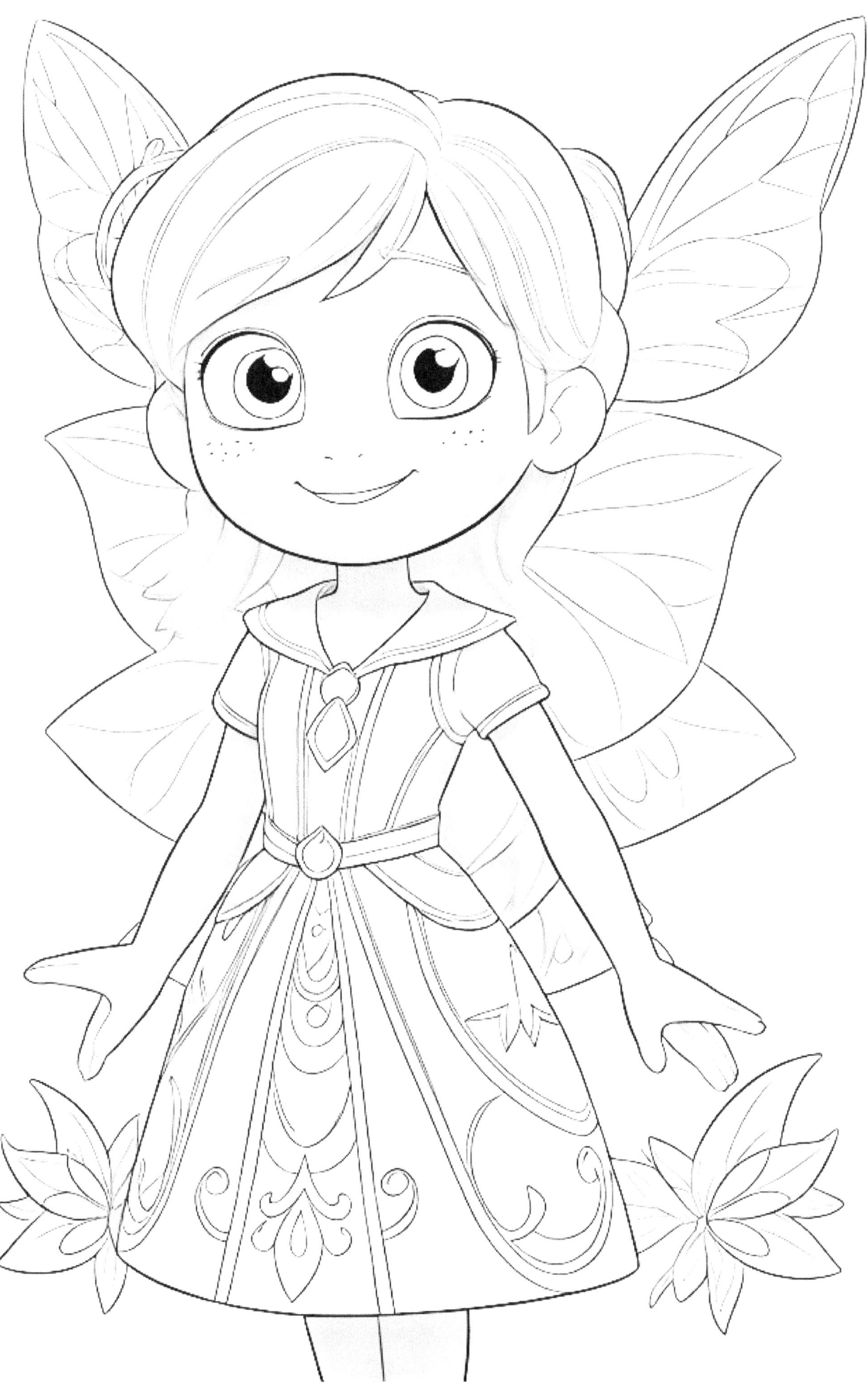

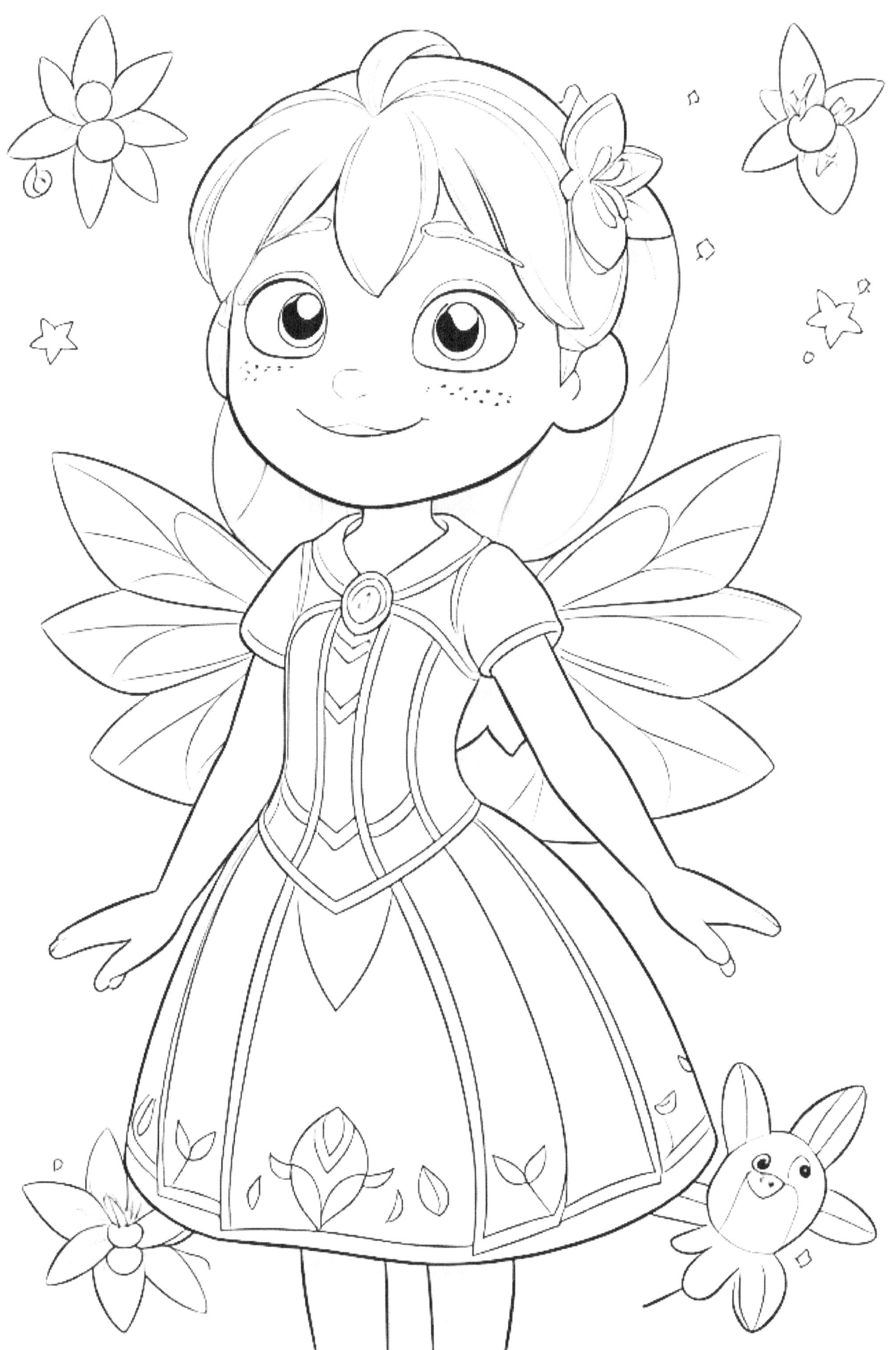

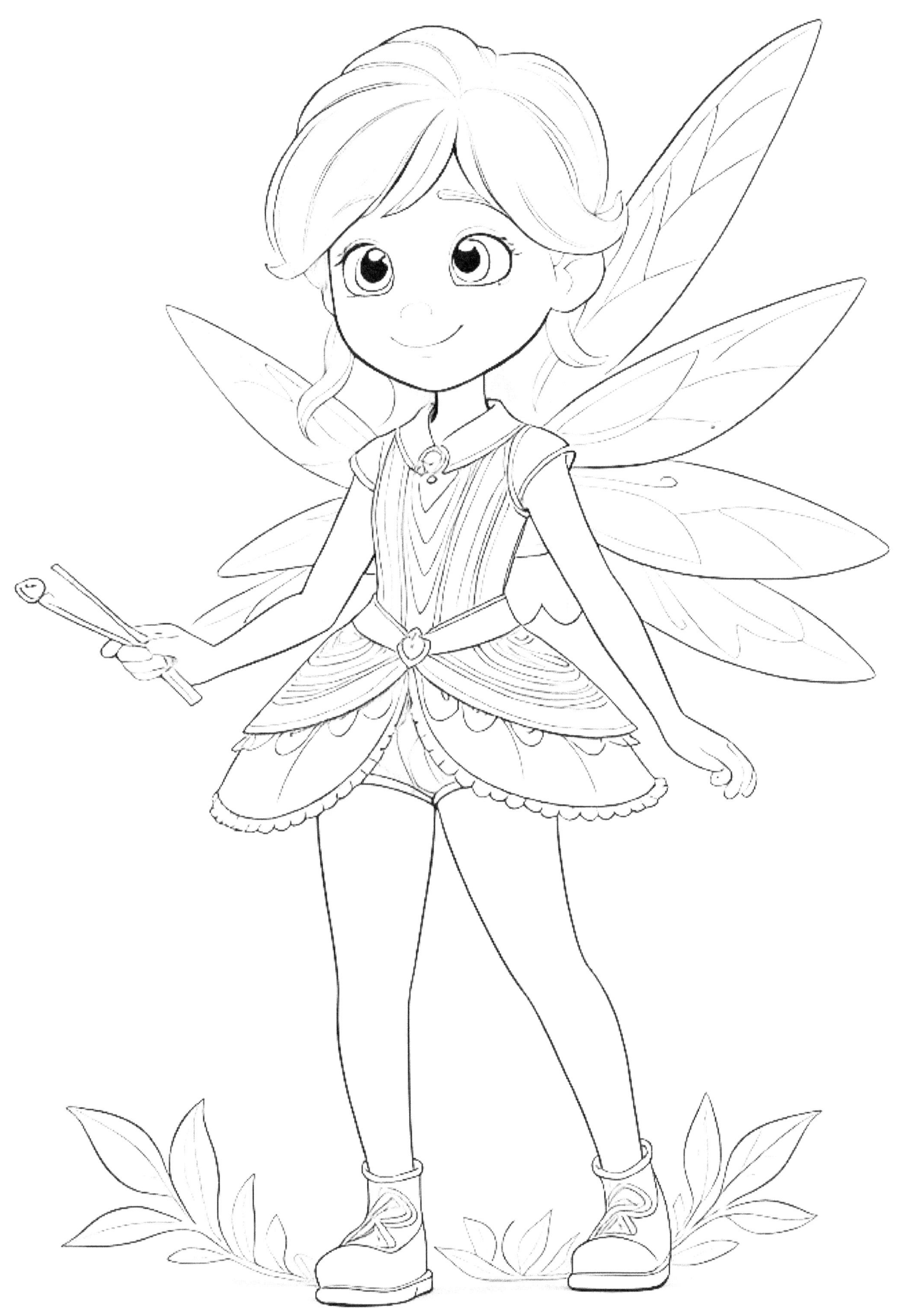

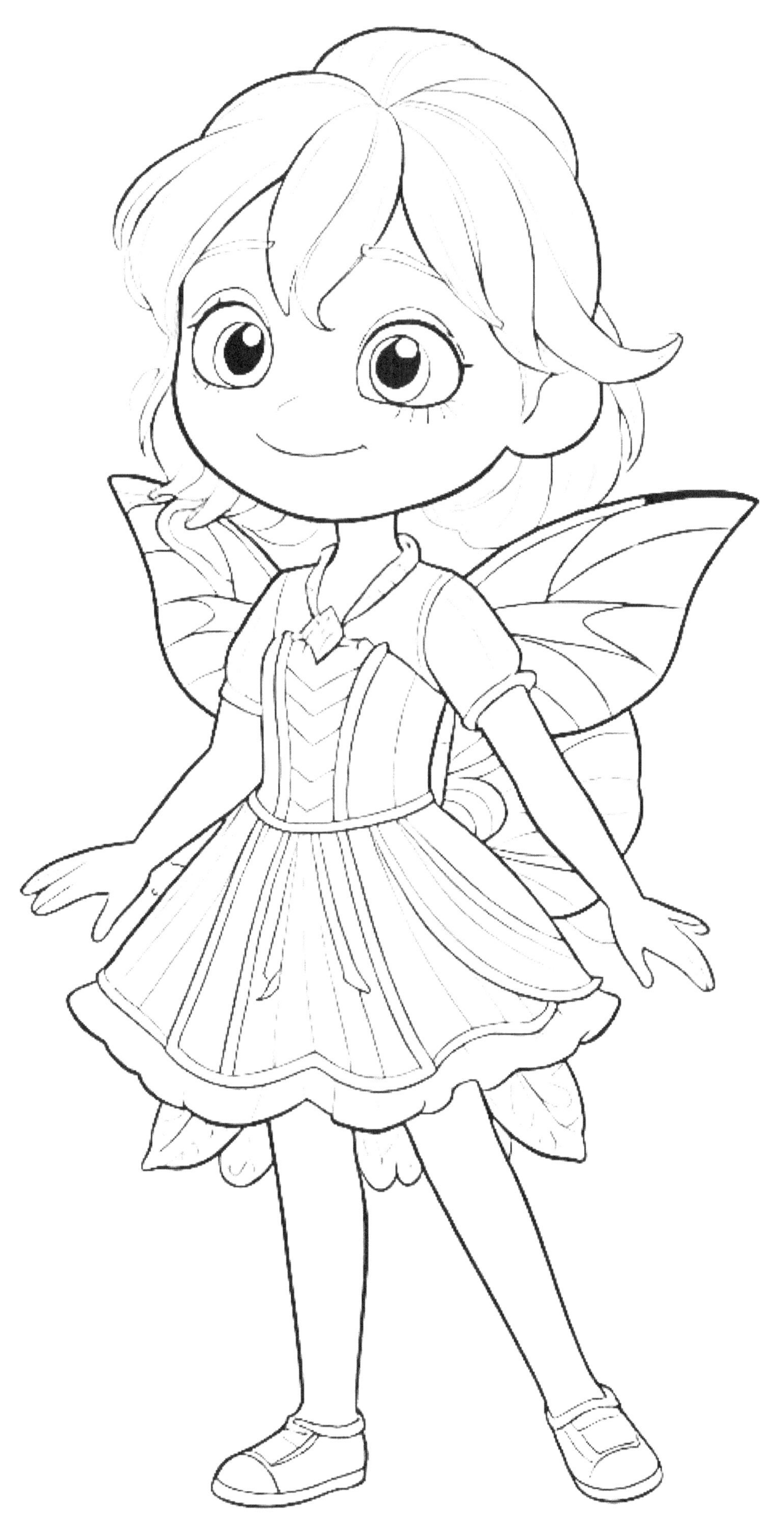

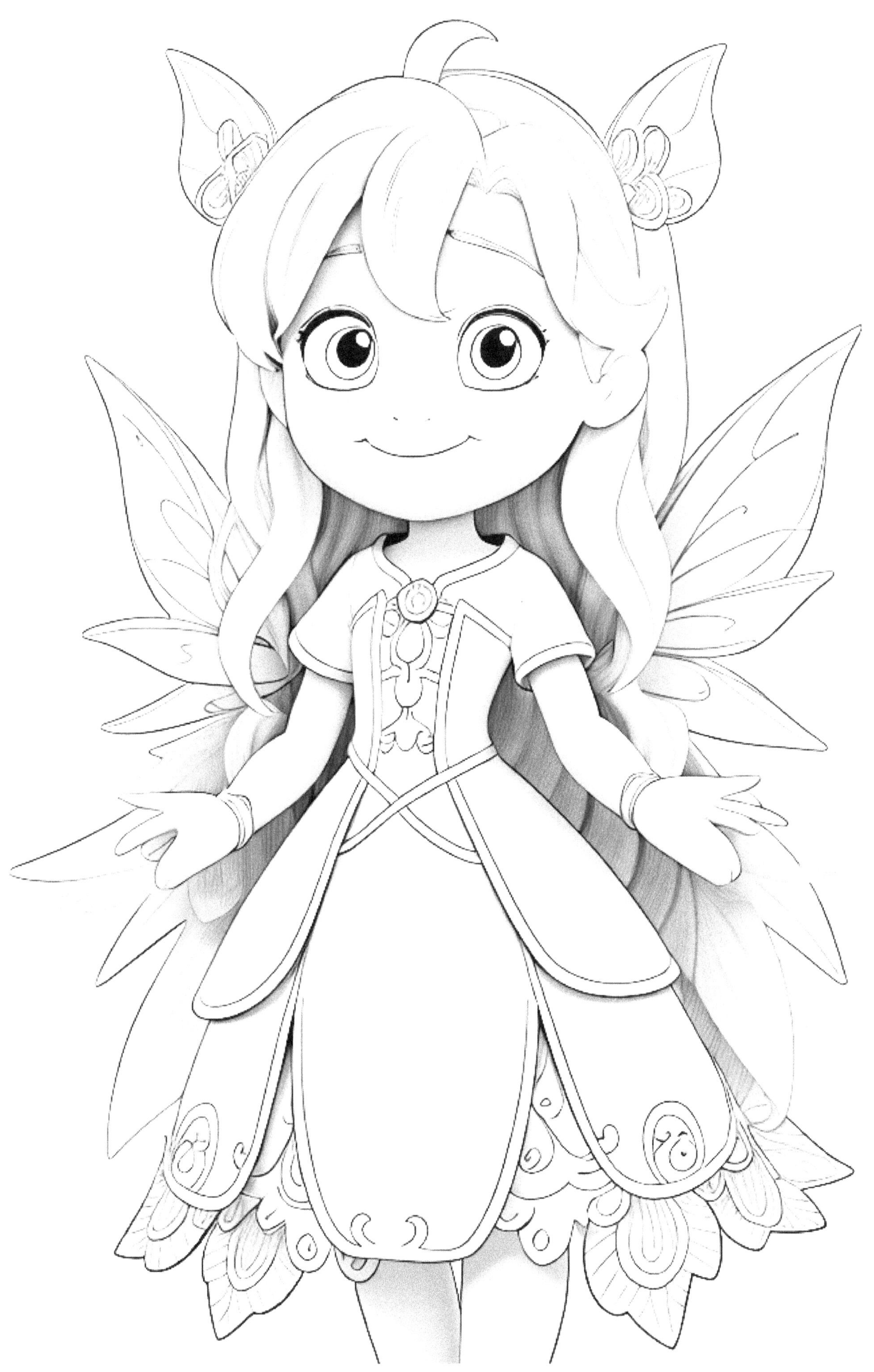

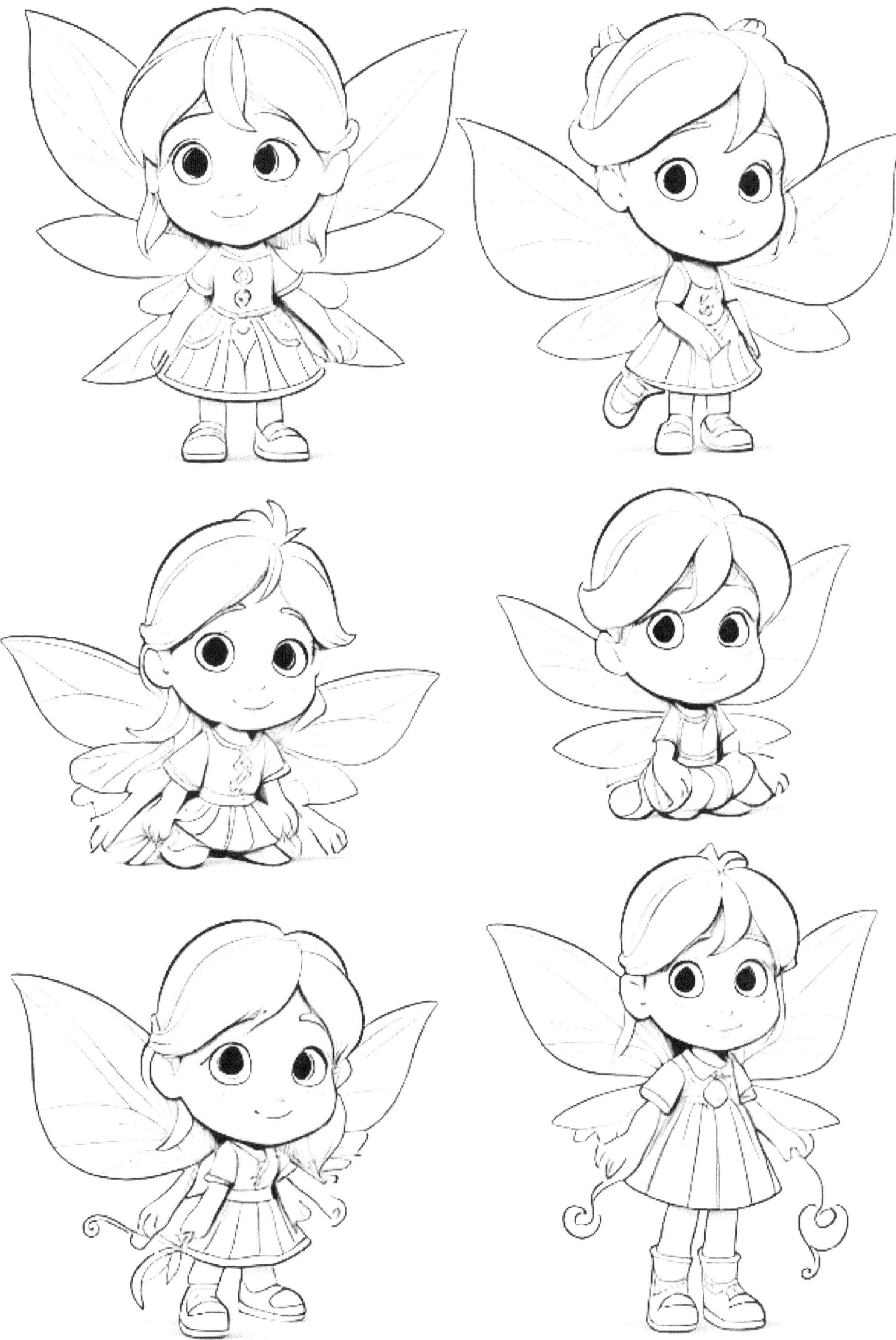

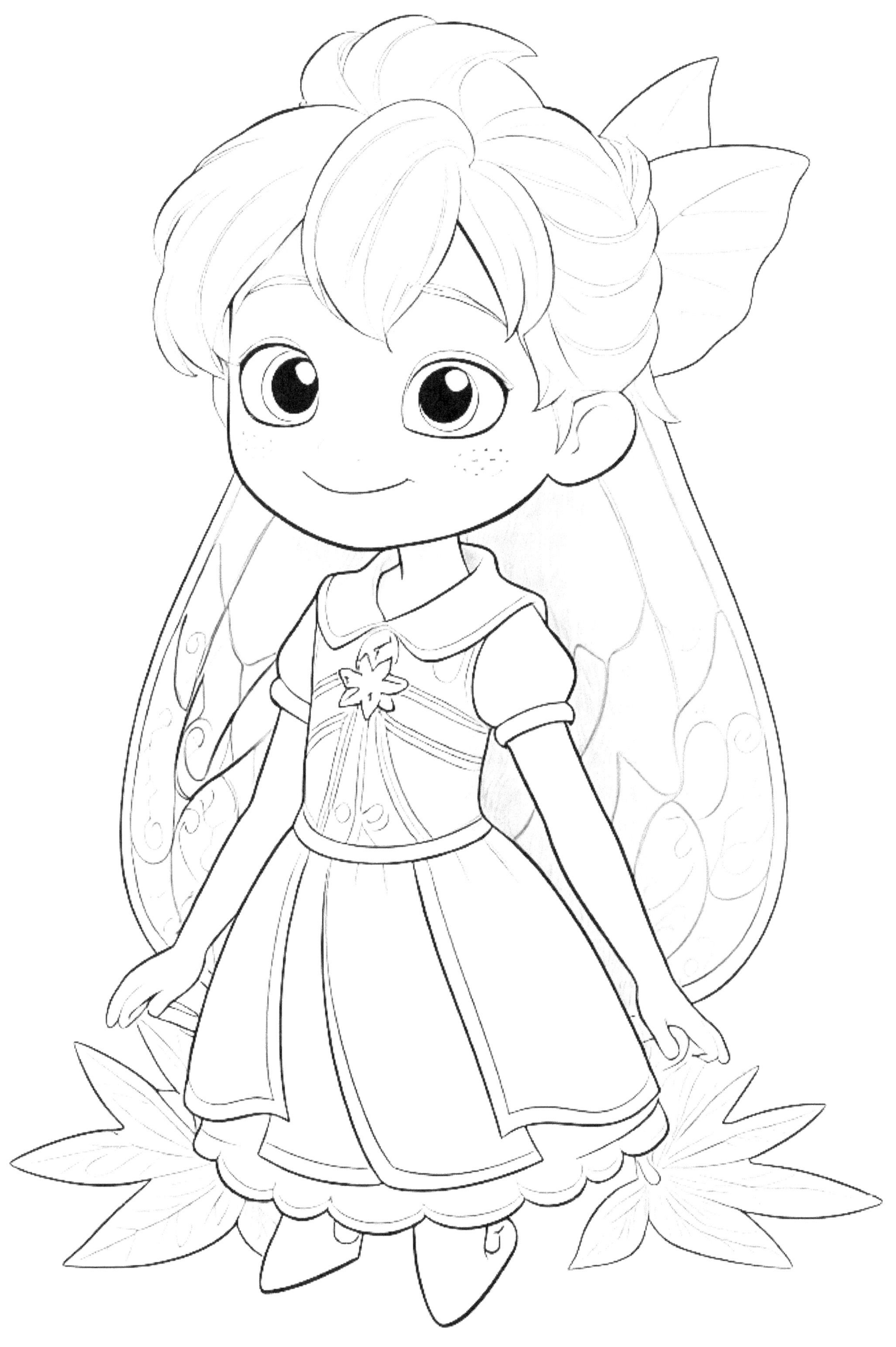

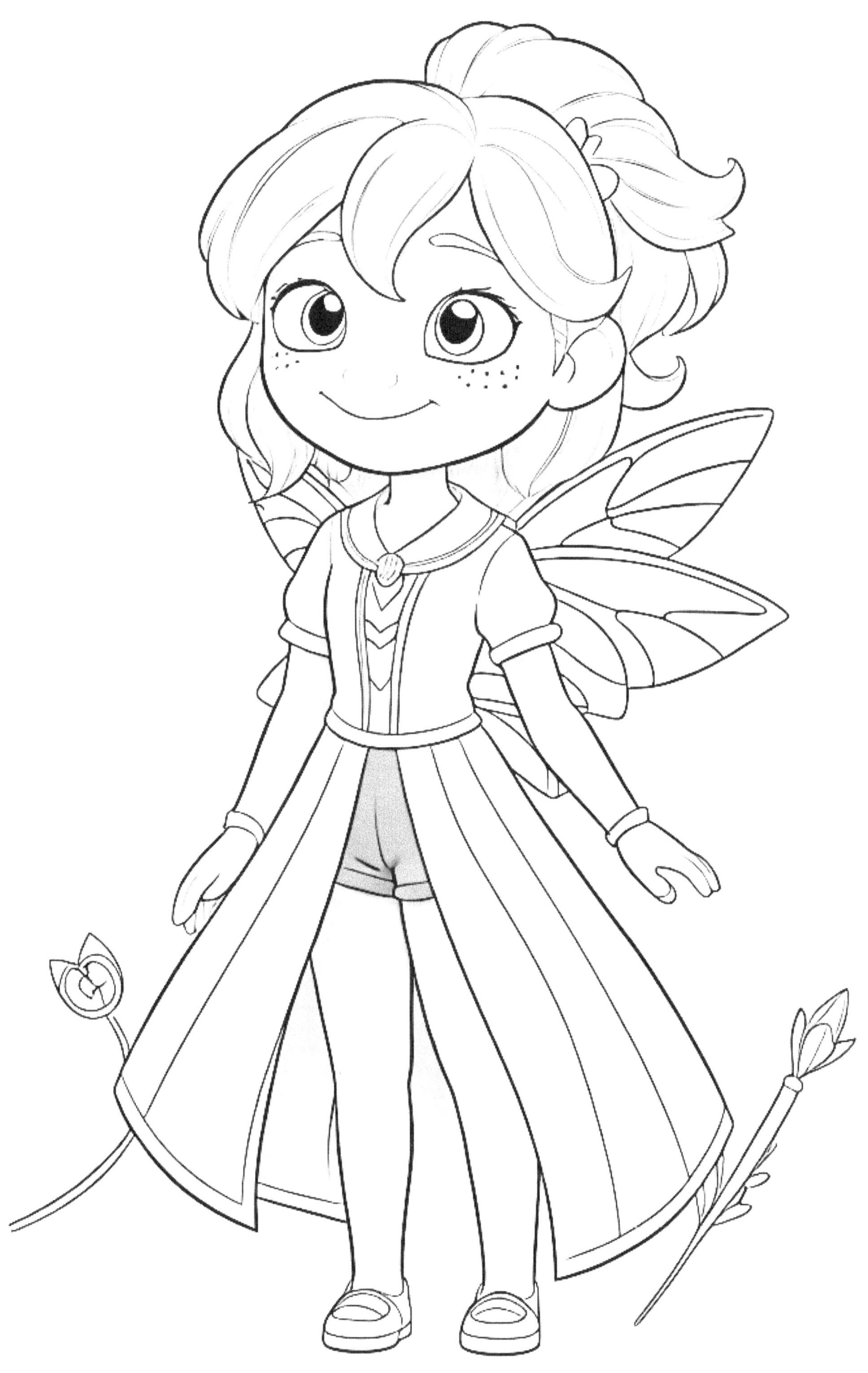

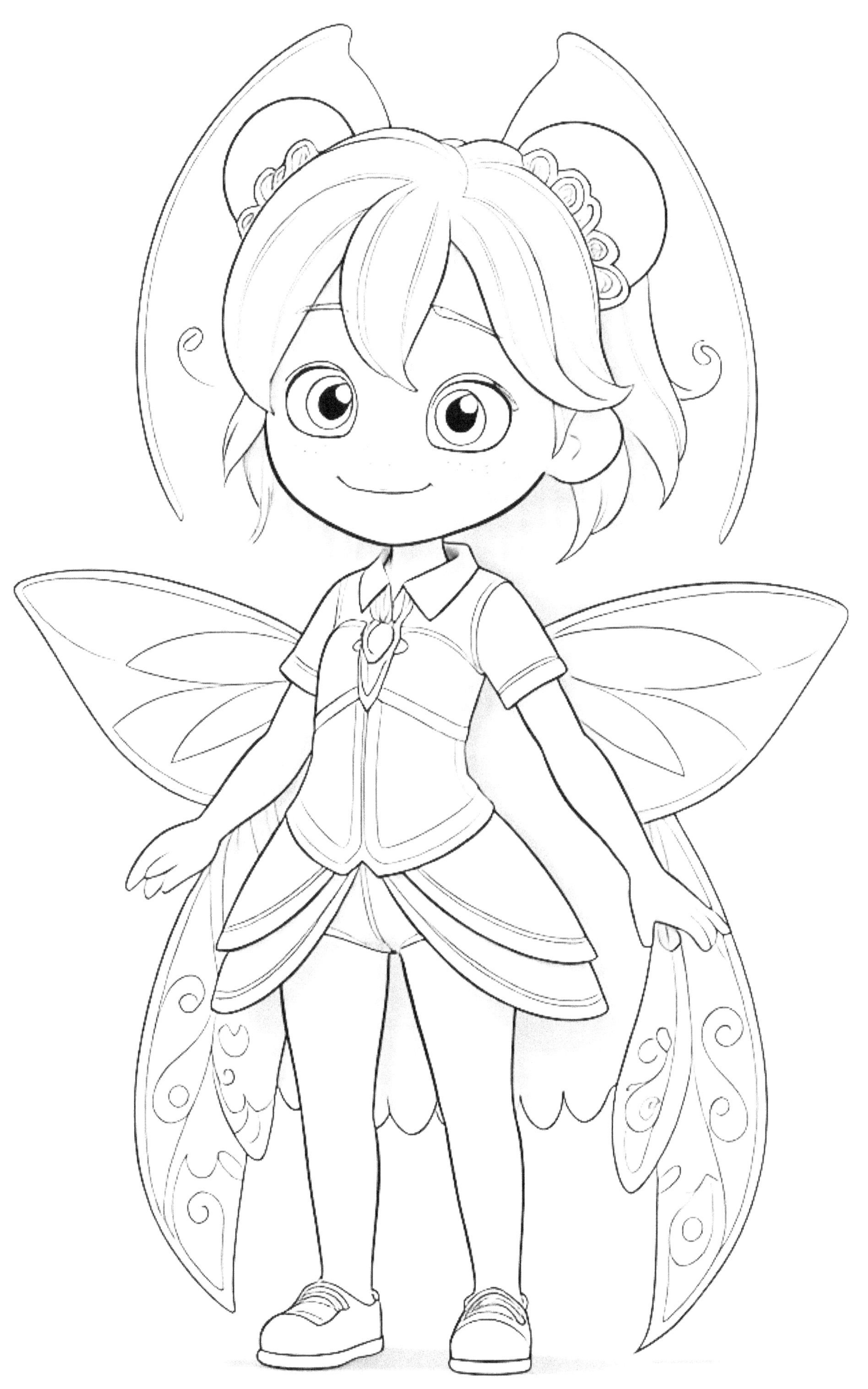

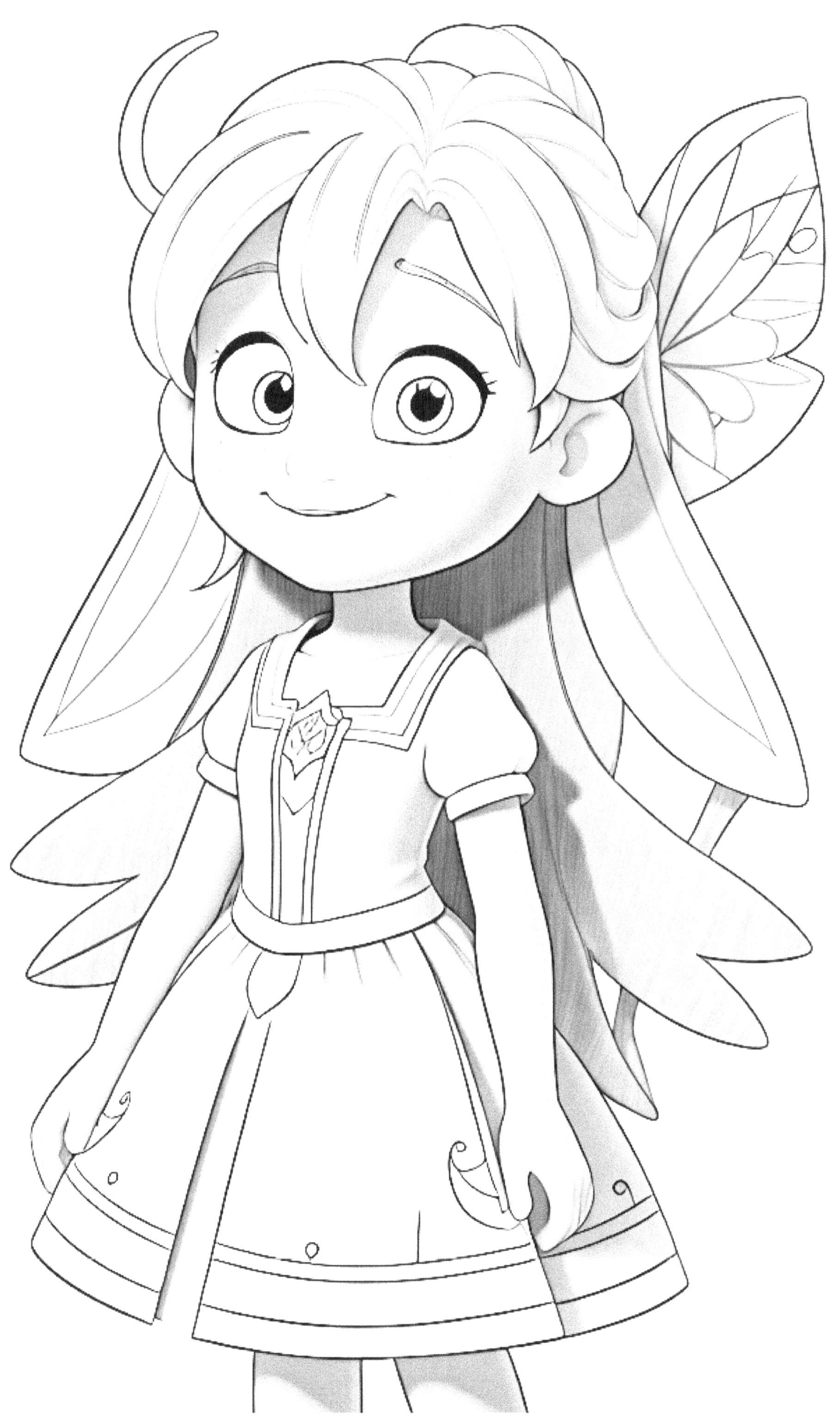

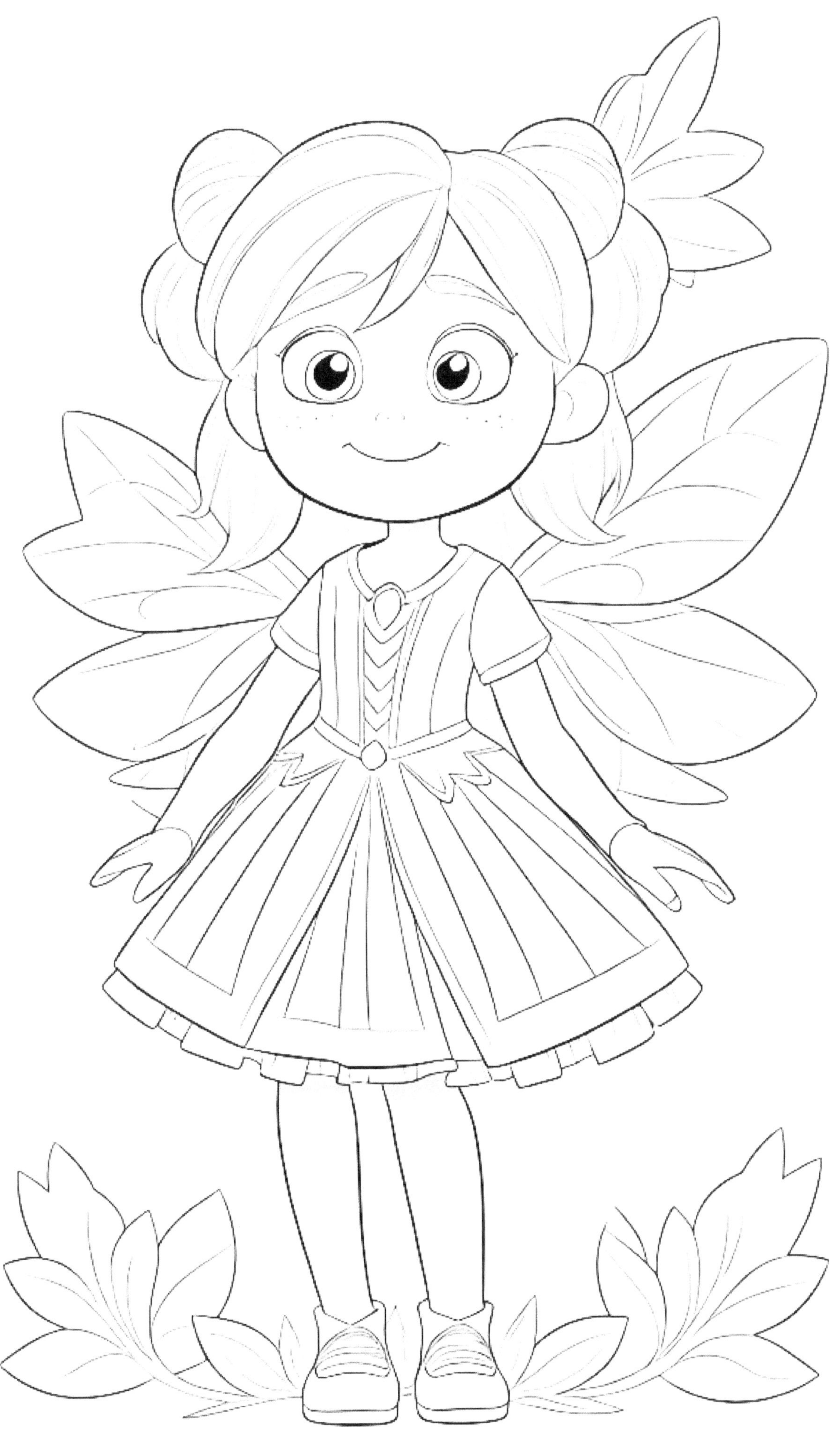

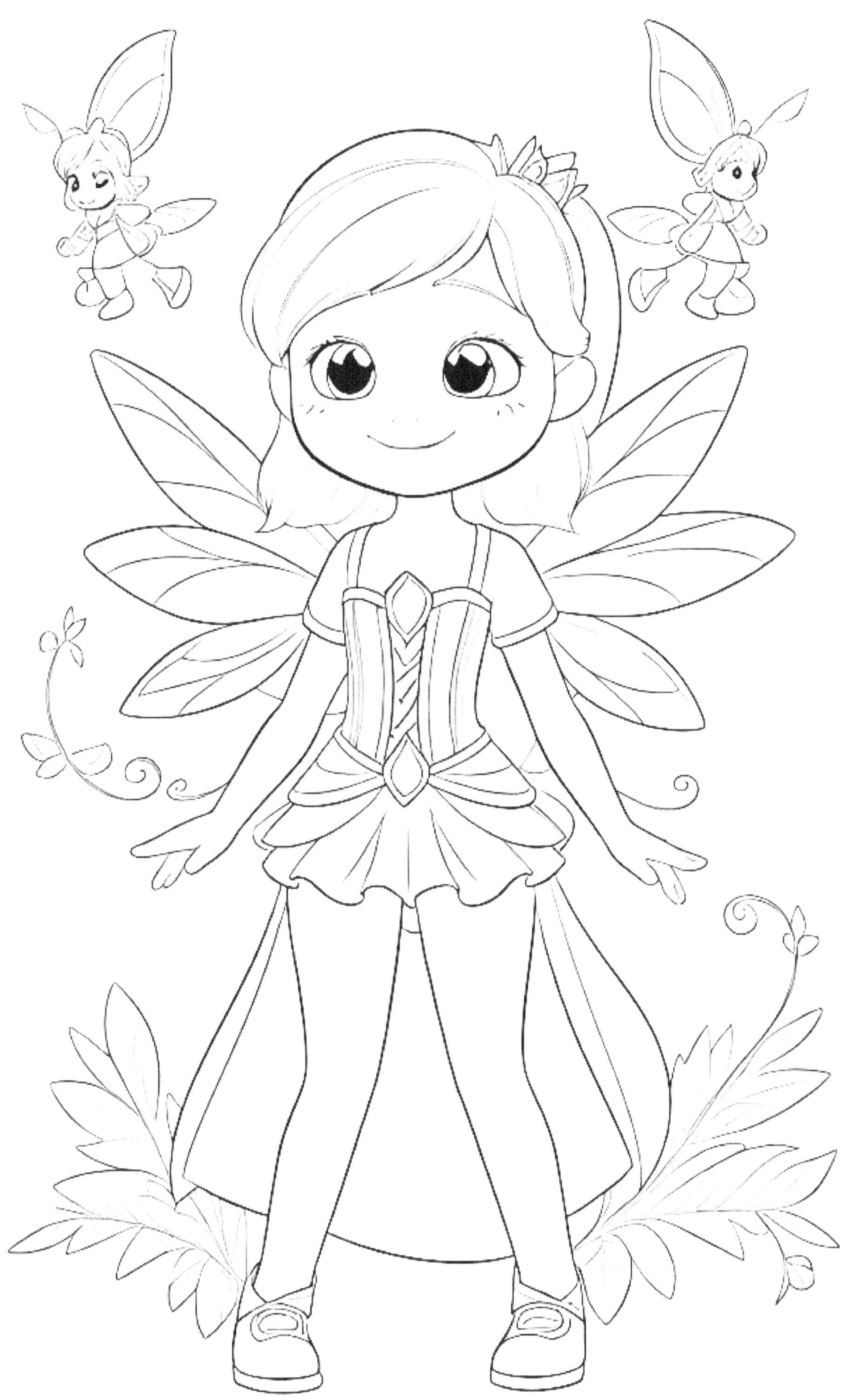

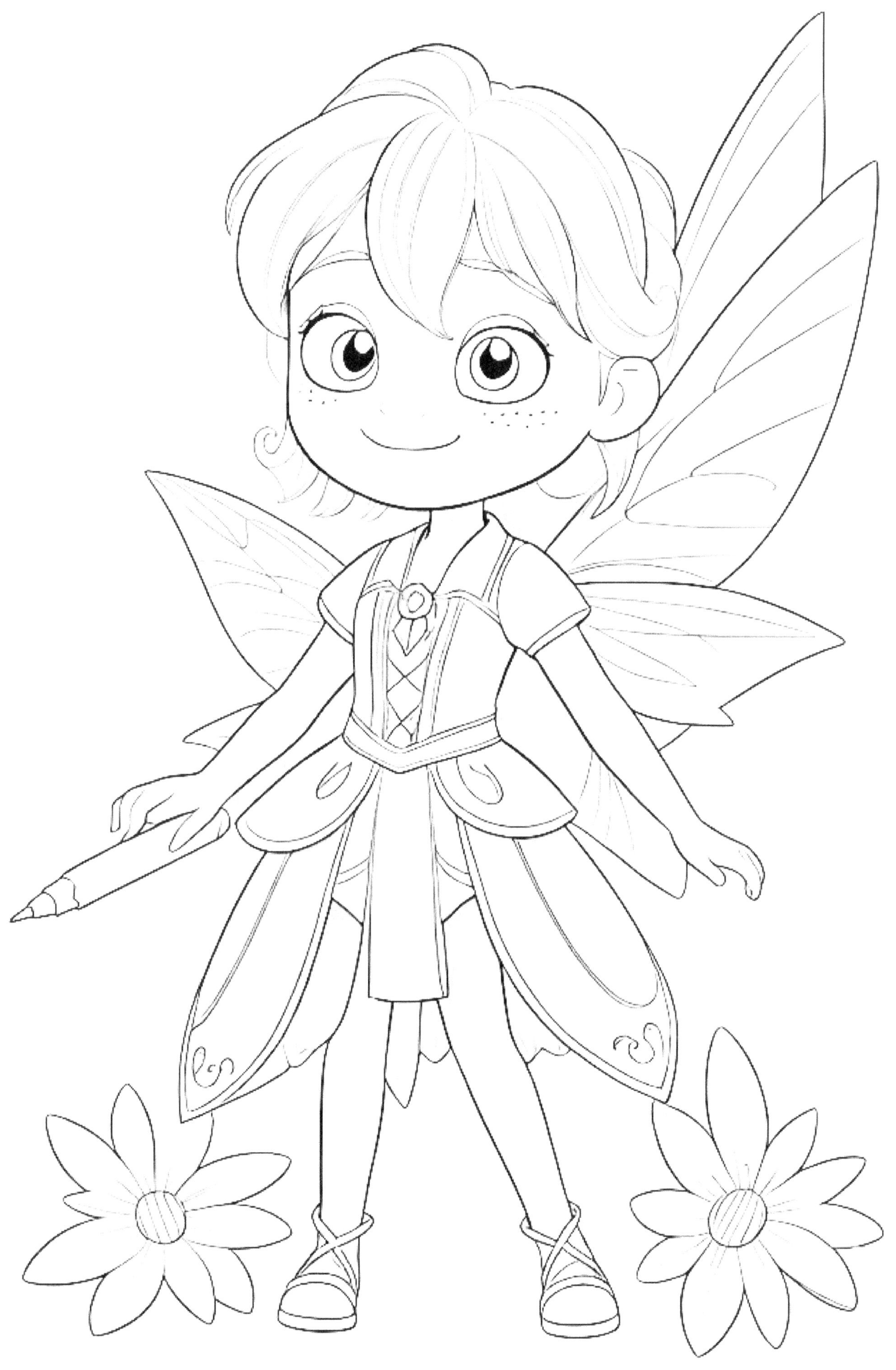

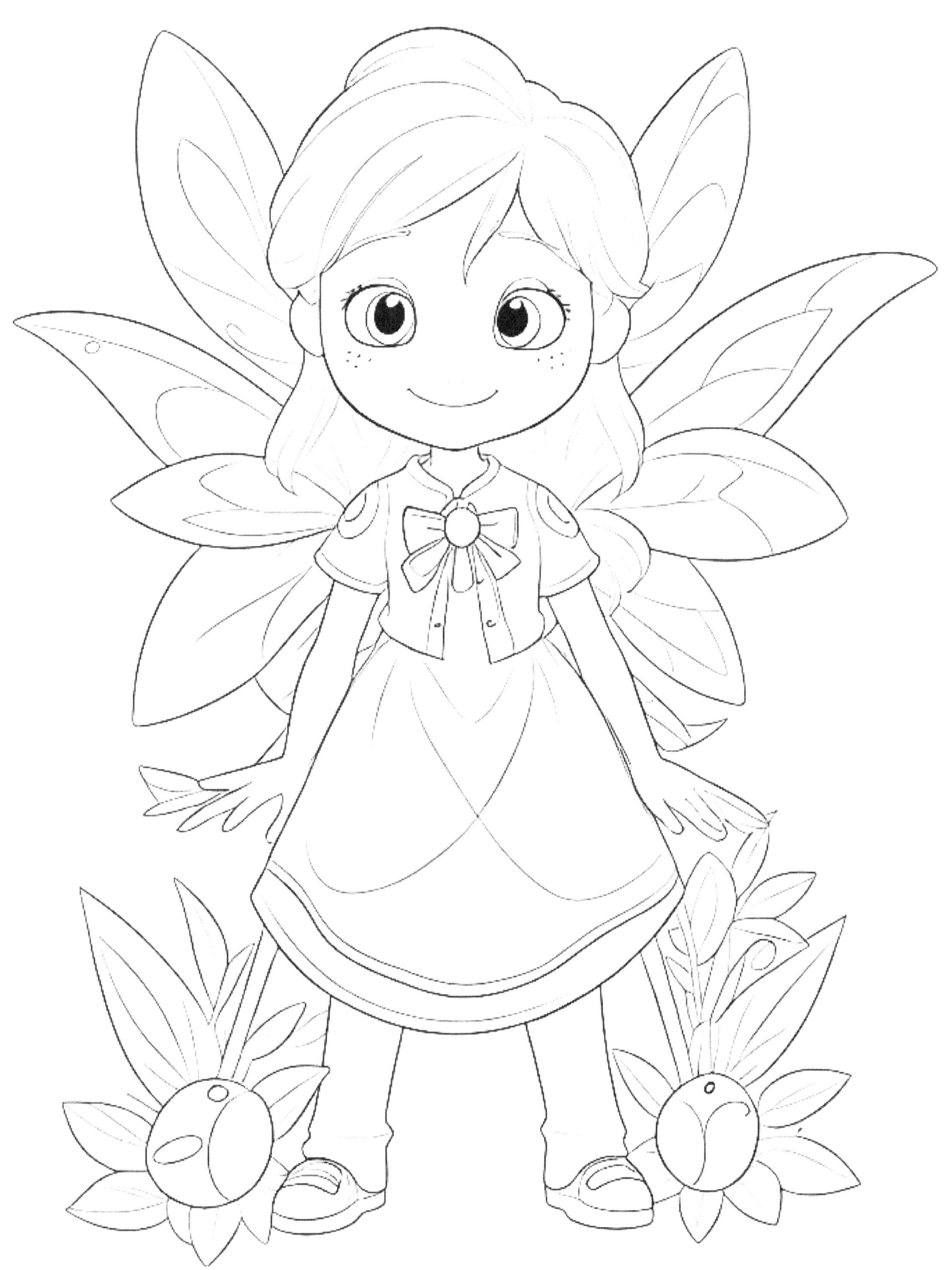

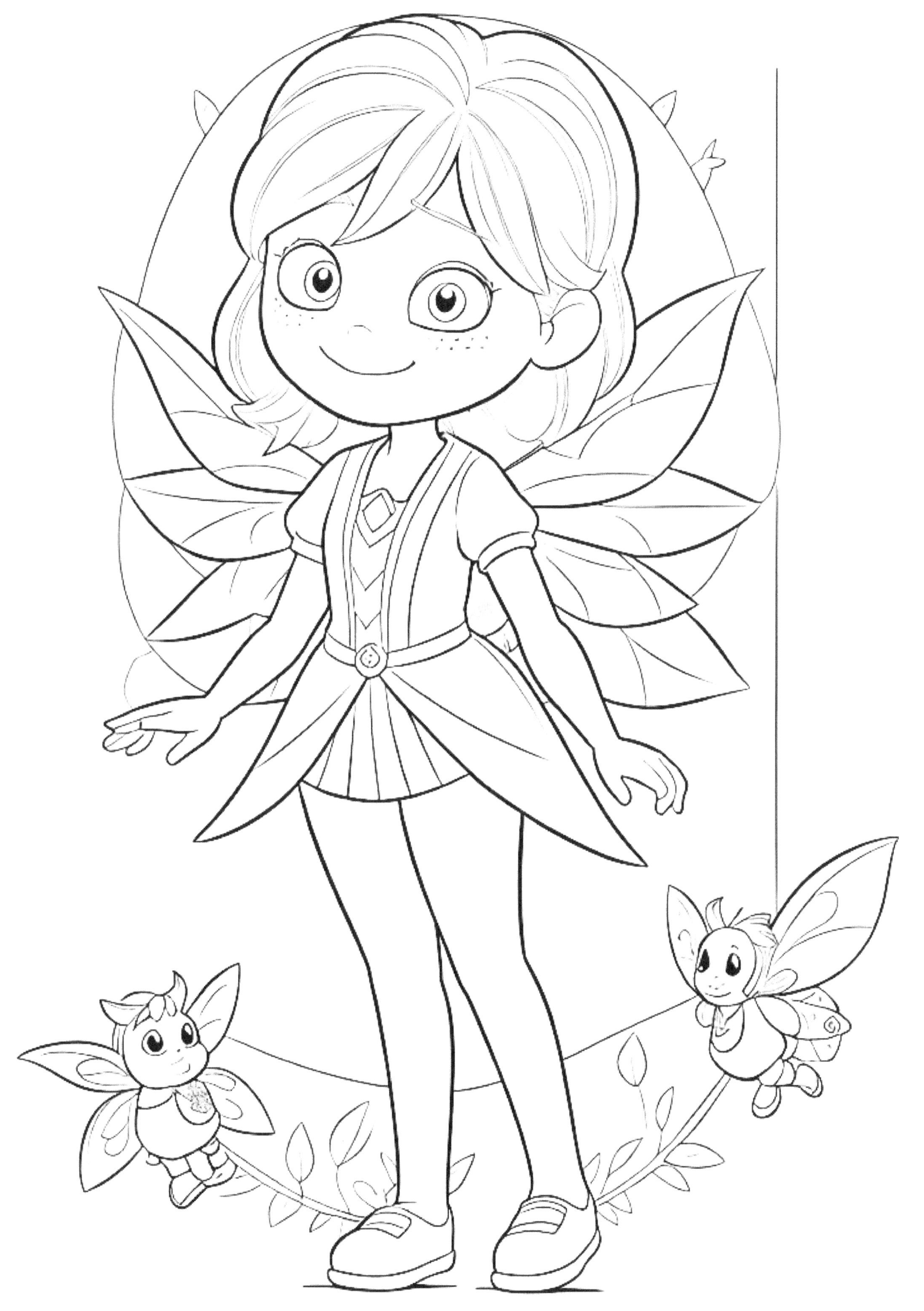

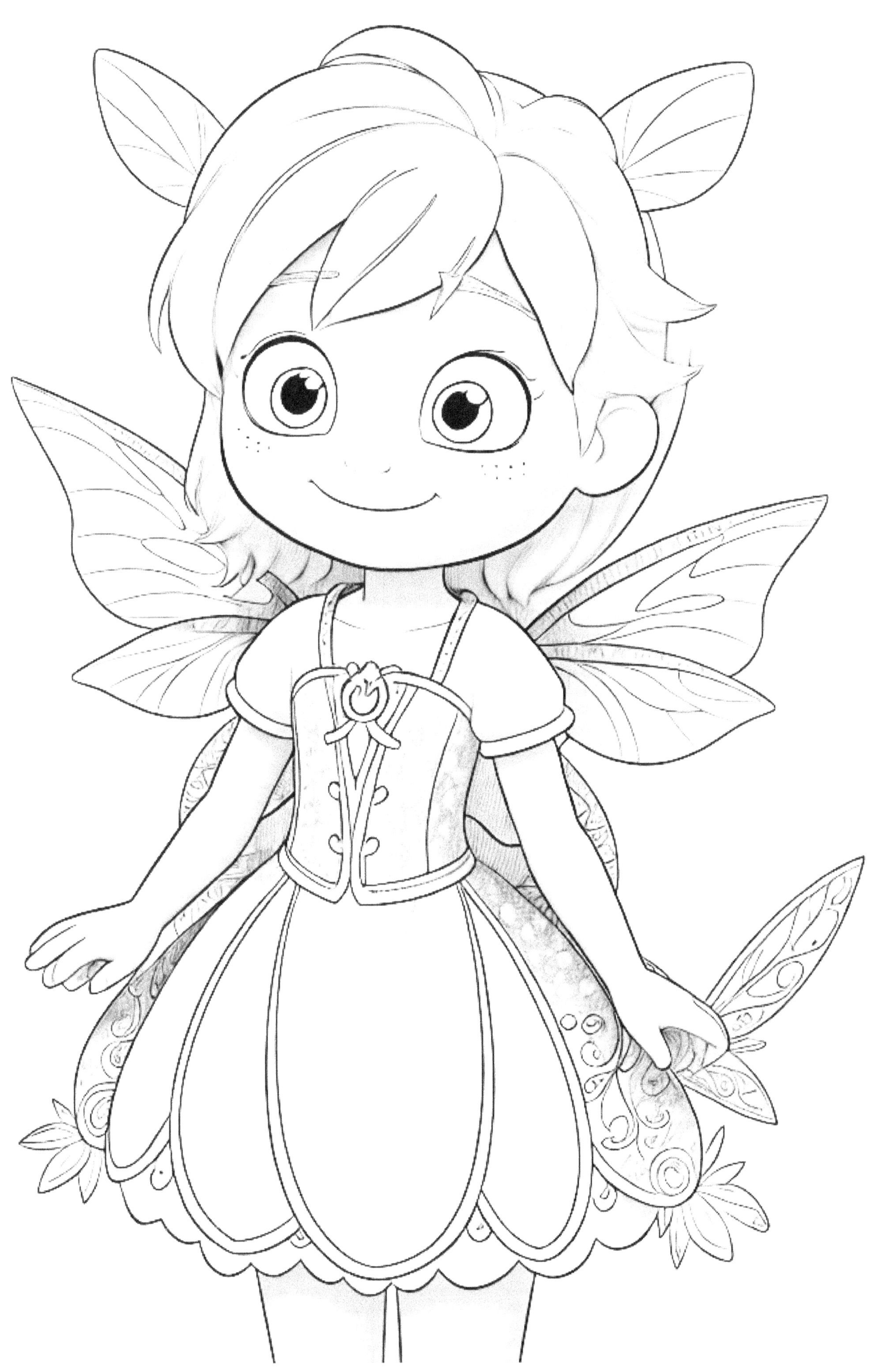

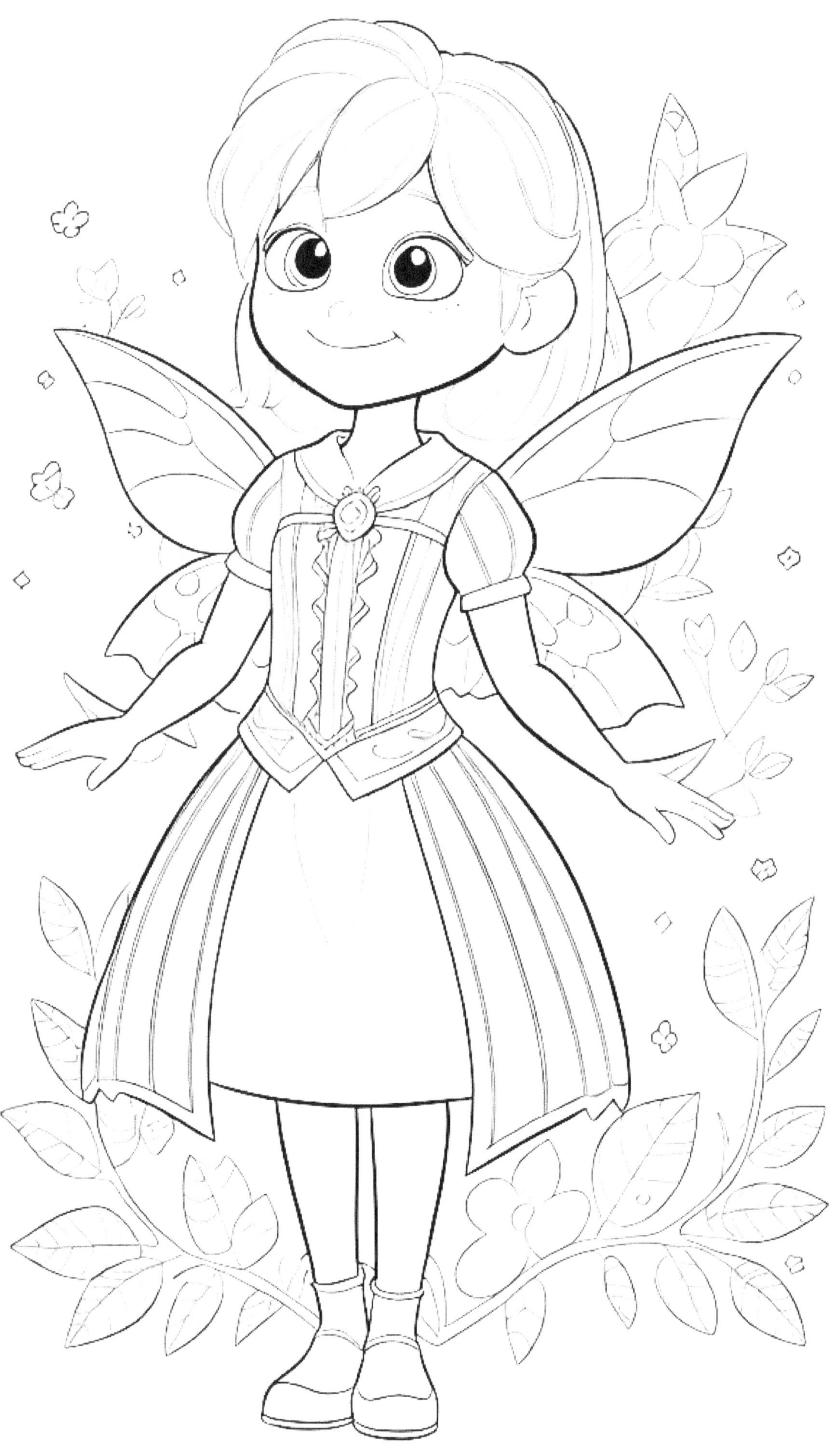

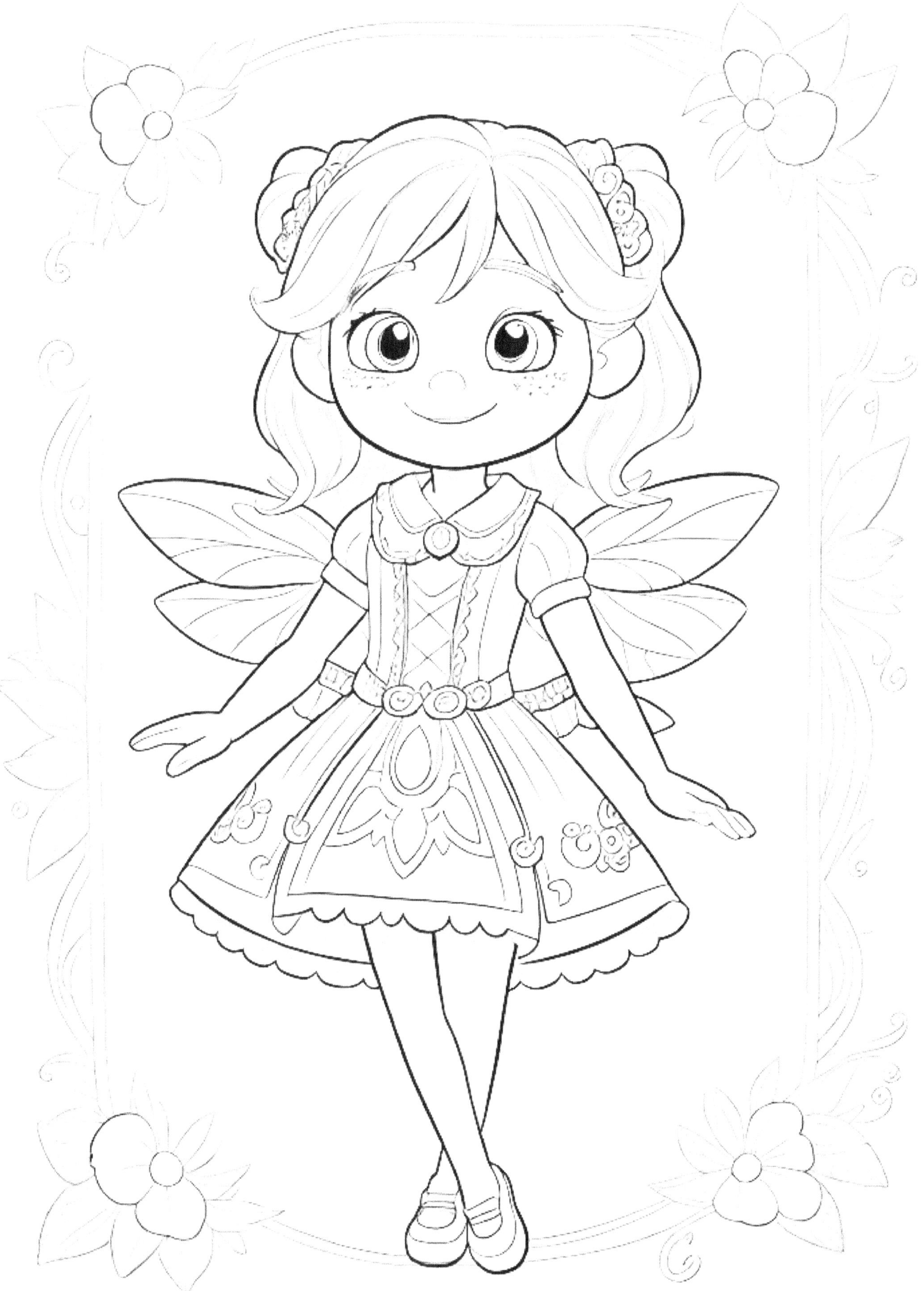

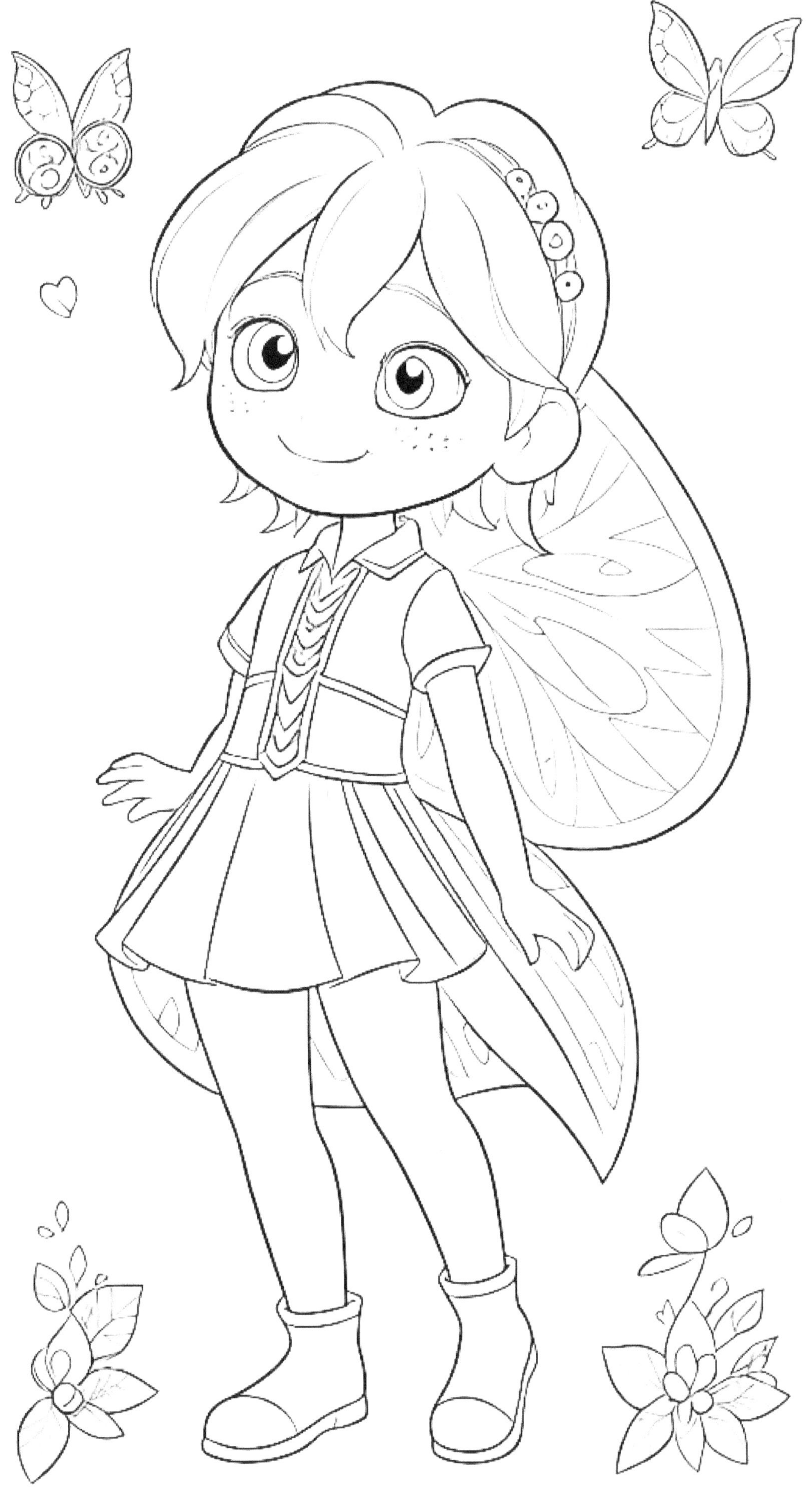

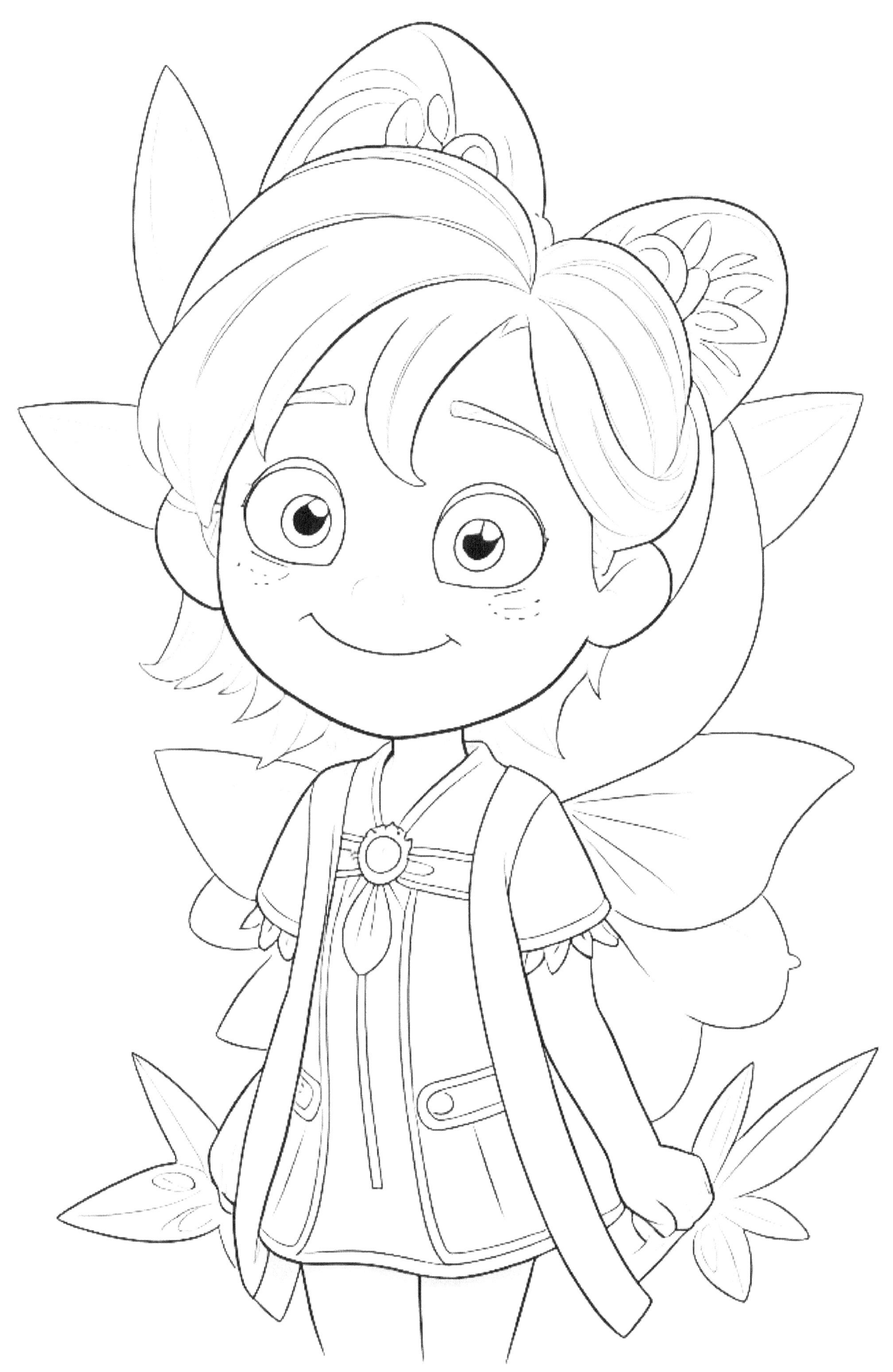

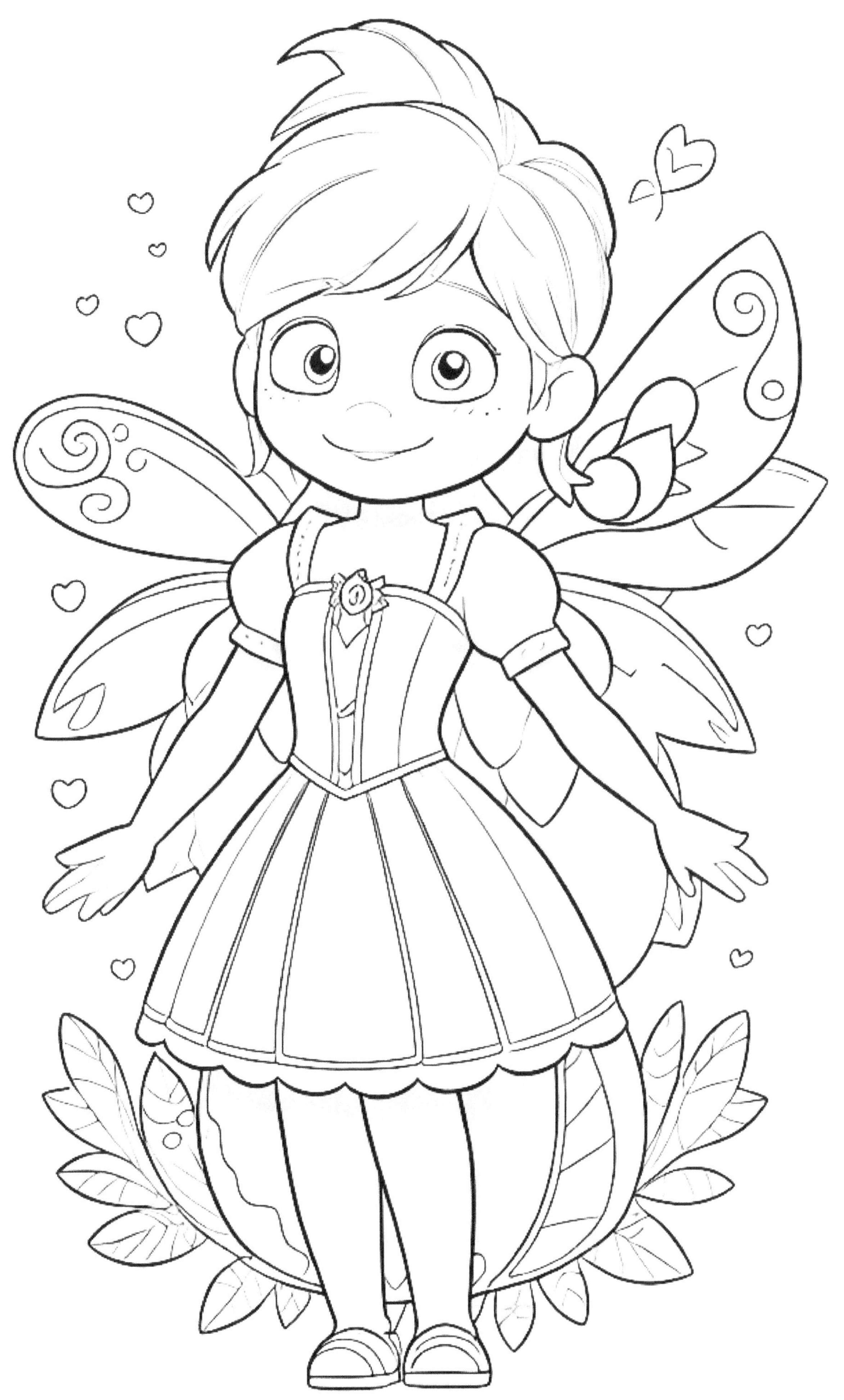

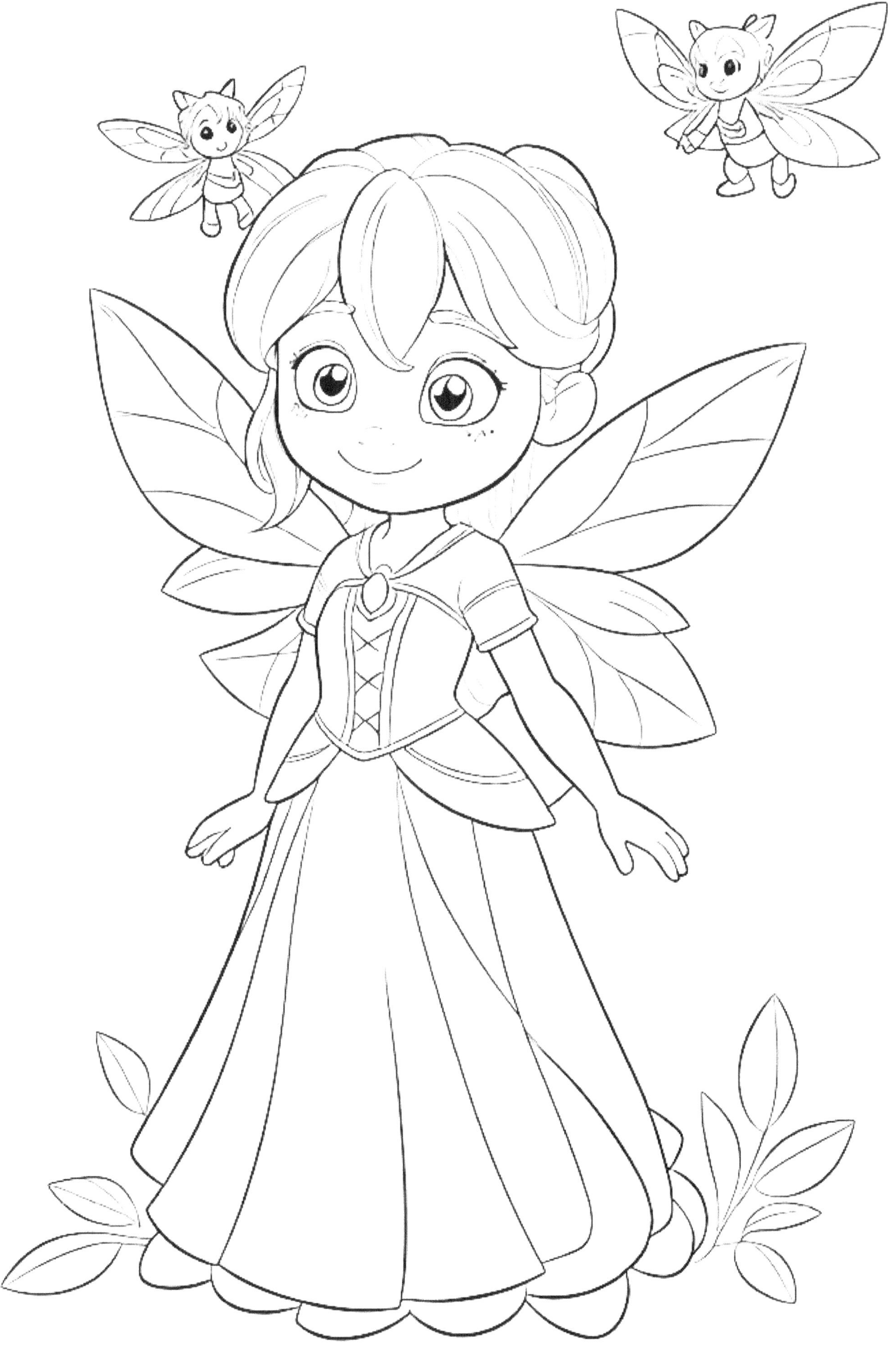

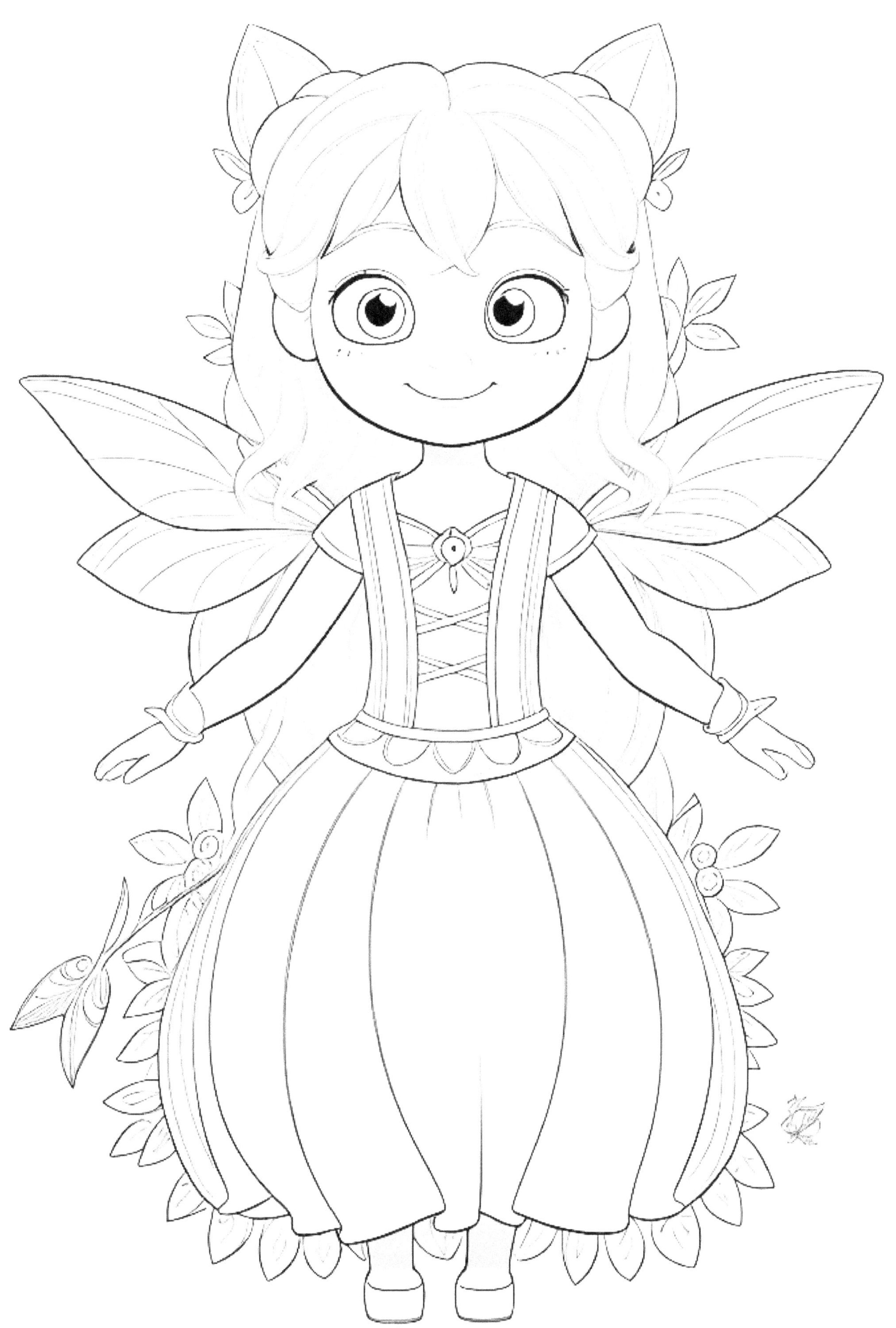